THE WHITE LINEN NURSE

Eleanor Hallowell Abbott

The White Linen Nurse

Eleanor Hallowell Abbott

PO Box 2211
Fairfield, IA 52556
www.1stworldlibrary.com
First Edition

LCCN: 2006935215

Softcover ISBN: 1-4218-2468-X
Hardcover ISBN: 1-4218-2368-3
eBook ISBN: 1-4218-2568-6

1st World Library Literary Society

Giving Back to the World

"If you want to work on the core problem, it's early school literacy."

- James Barksdale, former CEO of Netscape

"No skill is more crucial to the future of a child, or to a democratic and prosperous society, than literacy."

- Los Angeles Times

Literacy... means far more than learning how to read and write... The aim is to transmit... knowledge and promote social participation."

- UNESCO

"Literacy is not a luxury, it is a right and a responsibility. If our world is to meet the challenges of the twenty-first century we must harness the energy and creativity of all our citizens."

- President Bill Clinton

"Parents should be encouraged to read to their children, and teachers should be equipped with all available techniques for teaching literacy, so the varying needs and capacities of individual kids can be taken into account."

- Hugh Mackay

TO MAURICE HOWE RICHARDSON

WHO LOVED ROMANCE ALMOST AS MUCH AS HE
LOVED SURGERY, THIS LITTLE STORY
IS AFFECTIONATELY DEDICATED IN TOKEN OF
TWO PERSONS' UNFADING MEMORIES

CHAPTER I

The White Linen Nurse was so tired that her noble expression ached.

Incidentally her head ached and her shoulders ached and her lungs ached and the ankle-bones of both feet ached quite excruciatingly. But nothing of her felt permanently incapacitated except her noble expression. Like a strip of lip-colored lead suspended from her poor little nose by two tugging wire-gray wrinkles her persistently conscientious sickroom smile seemed to be whanging aimlessly against her front teeth. The sensation certainly was very unpleasant.

Looking back thus on the three spine-curving, chest-cramping, foot-twinging, ether-scented years of her hospital training, it dawned on the White Linen Nurse very suddenly that nothing of her ever had felt permanently incapacitated except her noble expression!

Impulsively she sprang for the prim white mirror that capped her prim white bureau and stood staring up into her own entrancing, bright-colored Novia Scotian reflection with tense and unwonted interest.

Except for the unmistakable smirk which fatigue had clawed into her plastic young mouth-lines there was certainly nothing special the matter with what she saw.

"Perfectly good face!" she attested judicially with no more than common courtesy to her progenitors. "Perfectly good and tidy looking face! If only - if only -" her breath caught a trifle. "If only - it didn't look so disgustingly noble and - hygienic - and dollish!"

All along the back of her neck little sharp prickly pains began suddenly to sting and burn.

"Silly - simpering - pink and white puppet!" she scolded squintingly, "I'll teach you how to look like a real girl!"

Very threateningly she raised herself to her tiptoes and thrust her glowing, corporeal face right up into the moulten, elusive, quick-silver face in the mirror. Pink for pink, blue for blue, gold for gold, dollish smirk for dollish smirk, the mirror mocked her seething inner fretfulness.

"Why - darn you!" she gasped. "Why - darn you! Why, you looked more human than that when you left the Annapolis Valley three years ago! There were at least - tears in your face then, and - cinders, and - your mother's best advice, and the worry about the mortgage, and - and - the blush of Joe Hazeltine's kiss!"

Furtively with the tip of her index-finger she started to search her imperturbable pink cheek for the spot where Joe Hazeltine's kiss had formerly flamed.

"My hands are all right, anyway!" she acknowledged with infinite relief. Triumphantly she raised both strong, stub-fingered, exaggeratedly executive hands to the level of her childish blue eyes and stood surveying the mirrored effect with ineffable satisfaction. "Why my hands are - dandy!" she gloated. "Why they're perfectly - dandy! Why they're wonderful! Why they're -." Then suddenly and fearfully she gave a shrill little scream. "But they don't go with my silly doll-face!" she cried. "Why, they don't! They don't! They go with the Senior Surgeon's scowling Heidelberg eyes! They go with the Senior Surgeon's grim gray jaw! They go with the -!

Oh! what shall I do? What shall I do?"

Dizzily, with her stubby finger-tips prodded deep into every jaded facial muscle that she could compass, she staggered towards the air, and dropping down into the first friendly chair that bumped against her knees, sat staring blankly out across the monotonous city roofs that flanked her open window, - trying very, very hard for the first time in her life, to consider the General-Phenomenon-of-Being-a-Trained-Nurse.

All around and about her, inexorable as anesthesia, horrid as the hush of tomb or public library, lurked the painfully unmistakable sense of institutional restraint. Mournfully to her ear from some remote kitcheny region of pots and pans a browsing spoon tinkled forth from time to time with soft-muffled resonance. Up and down every clammy white corridor innumerable young feet, born to prance and stamp, were creeping stealthily to and fro in rubber-heeled whispers. Along the somber fire-escape just below her windowsill, like a covey of snubbed doves, six or eight of her classmates were cooing and crooning together with excessive caution concerning the imminent graduation exercises that were to take place at eight o'clock that very evening. Beyond her dreariest ken of muffled voices, beyond her dingiest vista of slate and brick, on a far faint hillside, a far faint streak of April green went roaming jocundly skyward. Altogether sluggishly, as though her nostrils were plugged with warm velvet, the smell of spring and ether and scorched mutton-chops filtered in and out, in and out, in and out, of her abnormally jaded senses.

Taken all in all it was not a propitious afternoon for any girl as tired and as pretty as the White Linen Nurse to be considering the general phenomenon of anything - except April!

In the real country, they tell me, where the Young Spring runs wild and bare as a nymph through every dull brown wood and hay-gray meadow, the blasé farmer-lad will not even lift his eyes from the plow to watch the pinkness of her passing. But here in the prudish brick-minded city where the Young Spring at her friskiest is nothing more audacious than a sweltering, winter-swathed madcap, who has impishly essayed some fine morning to tiptoe down street in her soft, sloozily, green, silk-stockinged feet, the whole hob-nailed population reels back aghast and agrin before the most innocent flash of the rogue's green-veiled toes. And then, suddenly snatching off its own cumbersome winter foot-habits, goes chasing madly after her, in its own prankish, vari-colored socks.

Now the White Linen Nurse's socks were black, and cotton at that, a combination incontestably sedate. And the White Linen Nurse had waded barefoot through too many posied country pastures to experience any ordinary city thrill over the sight of a single blade of grass pushing scarily through a crack in the pavement, or puny, concrete-strangled maple tree flushing wanly to the smoky sky. Indeed for three hustling, square-toed, rubber-heeled city years the White Linen Nurse had never even stopped to notice whether the season was flavored with frost or thunder. But now, unexplainably, just at the end of it all, sitting innocently there at her own prim little bed-room window, staring innocently out across indomitable roof-tops, - with the crackle of glory and diplomas already ringing in her ears, - she heard, instead, for the first time in her life, the gaily dare-devil voice of the spring, a hoydenish challenge flung back at her, leaf-green, from the crest of a winter-scarred hill.

"Hello, White Linen Nurse!" screamed the saucy city spring. "Hello, White Linen Nurse! Take off your homely starched collar! Or your silly candy-box cap! Or any other thing that feels maddeningly artificial! And come out! And be very wild!"

Like a puppy dog cocking its head towards some strange, unfamiliar sound, the White Linen Nurse cocked her head towards the lure of the green-crested hill. Still wrestling conscientiously with the General-Phenomenon-of-Being-a-Trained-Nurse she found her collar suddenly very tight, the tiny cap inexpressibly heavy and vexatious. Timidly she removed the collar - and found that the removal did not rest her in the slightest. Equally timidly she removed the cap - and found that even that removal did not rest her in the slightest. Then very, very slowly, but very, very permeatingly and completely, it dawned on the White Linen Nurse that never while eyes were blue, and hair gold, and lips red, would she ever find rest again until she had removed her noble expression!

With a jerk that started the pulses in her temples throbbing like two toothaches she straightened up in her chair. All along the back of her neck the little blonde curls began to crisp very ticklingly at their roots.

Still staring worriedly out over the old city's slate-gray head to that inciting prance of green across the farthest horizon she felt her whole being kindle to an indescribable passion of revolt against all Hushed Places. Seething with fatigue, smoldering with ennui, she experienced suddenly a wild, almost incontrollable impulse to sing, to shout, to scream from the housetops, to mock somebody, to defy everybody, to break laws, dishes, heads, - anything in fact that would break with a crash! And then at last, over the hills and far away, with all the outraged world at her heels, to run! And run! And run! And run! And run! And laugh! Till her feet raveled out! And her lungs burst! And there was nothing more left of her at all, - ever - ever - any more!

Discordantly into this rapturously pagan vision of pranks and posies broke one of her room-mates all awhiff with ether, awhirr with starch.

Instantly with the first creak of the door-handle the White Linen Nurse was on her feet, breathless, resentful, grotesquely defiant.

"Get out of here, Zillah Forsyth!" she cried furiously. "Get out of here - quick! - and leave me alone! I want to think!"

Perfectly serenely the newcomer advanced into the room. With her pale, ivory-tinted cheeks, her great limpid brown eyes, her soft dark hair parted madonna-like across her beautiful brow, her whole face was like some exquisite, composite picture of all the saints of history. Her voice also was amazingly tranquil.

"Oh, Fudge!" she drawled. "What's eating you, Rae Malgregor? I won't either get out! It's my room just as much as it is yours! And Helene's just as much as it is ours! And besides," she added more briskly, "it's four o'clock now, and with graduation at eight and the dance afterwards, if we don't get our stuff packed up now, when in thunder shall we get it done?" Quite irrelevantly she began to laugh. Her laugh was perceptibly shriller than her speaking voice. "Say, Rae!" she confided. "That minister I nursed through pneumonia last winter wants me to pose as 'Sanctity' for a stained-glass window in his new church! Isn't he the softie?"

"Shall - you - do - it?" quizzed Rae Malgregor a trifle tensely.

"Shall I do it?" mocked the newcomer. "Well, you just watch me! Four mornings a week in June - at full week's wages? Fresh Easter lilies every day? White silk angel-robes? All the high-souls and high-paints kowtowing around me? Why it would be more fun than a box of monkeys! Sure I'll do it!"

Expeditiously as she spoke the newcomer reached up for the framed motto over her own ample mirror and yanking it down with one single tug began to busy herself adroitly with a snarl in the picture-cord. Like a with of willow yearning over a brook her slender figure curved to the task. Very scintillatingly the afternoon light seemed to brighten suddenly across her lap. *You'll Be a Long Time Dead!* glinted the mott o throughits sun-dazzled glass.

Still panting with excitement, still bristling with resentment, Rae Malgregor stood surveying the intrusion and the intruder. A dozen impertinent speeches were rioting in her mind. Twice her mouth opened and shut before she finally achieved the particular opprobrium that completely satisfied her.

"Bah! You look like a - Trained Nurse!" she blurted forth at last with hysterical triumph.

"So do you!" said the newcomer amiably.

With a little gasp of dismay Rae Malgregor sprang suddenly forward. Her eyes were flooded with tears.

"Why, that's just exactly what's the matter with me!" she cried. "My face is all worn out trying to look like a Trained Nurse! Oh, Zillah, how do you know you were meant to be a Trained Nurse? How does anybody know? Oh, Zillah! Save me! Save me!"

Languorously Zillah Forsyth looked up from her work, and laughed. Her laugh was like the accidental tinkle of sleighbells in mid-summer, vaguely disquieting, a shiver of frost across the face of a lily.

"Save you from what, you great big overgrown, tow-headed doll-baby?" she questioned blandly. "For Heaven's sake, the only thing you need is to go back to whatever toy-shop you came from and get a new head. What in Creation's the matter with you lately, anyway? Oh, of course, you've had rotten luck this past month, but what of it? That's the trouble with you country girls. You haven't got any stamina."

With slow, shuffling-footed astonishment Rae Malgregor stepped out into the center of the room. "Country girls," she repeated blankly. "Why, you're a country girl yourself!"

"I *am* not!" snapped Zillah Forsyth. "I'll have you understand that there are nine thousand people in the town I come from - and not a rube among them. Why I tended soda fountain in the swellest drug-store there a whole year before I even thought of taking up nursing. And I wasn't as green - when I was six months old - as you are now!"

Slowly with a soft-snuggling sigh of contentment she raised her slim white fingers to coax her dusky hair a little looser, a little farther down, a little more madonna-like across her sweet, mild forehead, then snatching out abruptly at a convenient shirt-waist began with extraordinary skill to apply its dangly lace sleeves as a protective bandage for the delicate glass-faced motto still in her lap, placed the completed parcel with inordinate scientific precision in the exact corner of her packing-box, and then went on very diligently, very zealously, to strip the men's photographs from the mirror on her bureau. There were twenty-seven photographs in all, and for each one she had already cut and prepared a small square of perfectly fresh, perfectly immaculate white tissue wrapping-paper. No one so transcendently fastidious, so exquisitely neat, in all her personal habits had ever trained in that particular hospital before.

Very soberly the doll-faced girl stood watching the men's pleasant paper countenances smooth away one by one into their chaste white veilings, until at last quite without warning she poked an accusing, inquisitive finger directly across Zillah Forsyth's shoulder.

"Zillah!" she demanded peremptorily. "All the year I've wanted to know! All the year every other girl in our class has wanted to know! Where did you ever get that picture of the Senior Surgeon? He never gave it to you in the world! He didn't! He didn't! He's not that kind!"

Deeply into Zillah Forsyth's pale, ascetic cheek dawned a most amazing dimple. "Sort of jarred you girls some, didn't it," she queried, "to see me strutting round with a photo of the Senior Surgeon?" The little cleft in her chin showed suddenly with almost startling distinctness. "Well, seeing it's you," she grinned, "and the year's all over, and there's nobody left that I can worry about it any more, I don't mind telling you in the least that I - bought it out of a photographer's show-case! There! Are you satisfied now?"

With easy nonchalance she picked up the picture in question

and scrutinized it shrewdly.

"Lord! What a face!" she attested. "Nothing but granite! Hack him with a knife and he wouldn't bleed but just chip off into pebbles!" With exaggerated contempt she shrugged her supple shoulders. "Bah! How I hate a man like that! There's no fun in him!" A little abruptly she turned and thrust the photograph into Rae Malgregor's hand. "You can have it if you want to," she said. "I'll trade it to you for that lace corset-cover of yours!"

Like water dripping through a sieve the photograph slid through Rae Malgregor's frightened fingers. With nervous apology she stooped and picked it up again and held it gingerly by one remotest corner. Her eyes were quite wide with horror.

"Oh, of course I'd like the - picture, well enough," she stammered. "But it wouldn't seem - exactly respectful to - to trade it for a corset-cover."

"Oh, very well," drawled Zillah Forsyth. "Tear it up then!"

Expeditiously with frank, non-sentimental fingers Rae Malgregor tore the tough cardboard across, and again across, and once again across, and threw the conglomerate fragments into the waste-basket. And her expression all the time was no more, no less, than the expression of a person who would infinitely rather execute his own pet dog or cat than risk the possible bungling of an outsider. Then like a small child trotting with infinite relief to its own doll-house she trotted over to her bureau, extracted the lace corset-cover, and came back with it in her hand to lean across Zillah Forsyth's shoulder again and watch the men's faces go slipping off into oblivion. Once again, abruptly without warning, she halted the process with a breathless exclamation.

"Oh, of course this waist is the only one I've got with ribbons in it," she asserted irrelevantly. "But I'm perfectly willing to trade it for that picture!" she pointed out with unmistakably explicit finger-tip.

Chucklingly Zillah Forsyth withdrew the special photograph from its half-completed wrappings.

"Oh! Him?" she said. "Oh, that's a chap I met on the train last summer. He's a brakeman or something. He's a -"

Perfectly unreluctantly Rae Malgregor dropped the fluff of lace and ribbons into Zillah's lap and reached out with cheerful voraciousness to annex the young man's picture to her somewhat bleak possessions. "Oh, I don't care a rap who he is," she interrupted briskly. "But he's sort of cute-looking, and I've got an empty frame at home just that odd size, and Mother's crazy for a new picture to stick up over the kitchen mantelpiece. She gets so tired of seeing nothing but the faces of people she knows all about."

Sharply Zillah Forsyth turned and stared up into the younger girl's face, and found no guile to whet her stare against.

"Well of all the ridiculous - unmitigated greenhorns!" she began. "Well - is that all you wanted him for? Why, I supposed you wanted to write to him! Why, I supposed -"

For the first time an expression not altogether dollish darkened across Rae Malgregor's garishly juvenile blondeness.

"Maybe I'm not quite as green as you think I am!" she flared up stormily. With this sharp flaring-up every single individual pulse in her body seemed to jerk itself suddenly into conscious activity again like the soft, plushy pound-pound-pound of a whole stocking-footed regiment of pain descending single file upon her for her hysterical undoing. "Maybe I've had a good deal more experience than you give me credit for!" she hastened excitedly to explain. "I tell you - I tell you I've been engaged!" she blurted forth with a bitter sort of triumph.

With a palpable flicker of interest Zillah Forsyth looked back across her shoulder. "Engaged? How many times?" she asked quite bluntly.

As though the whole monogamous groundwork of civilization was threatened by the question, Rae Malgregor's hands went clutching at her breast. "Why, once!" she gasped. "Why, once!"

Convulsively Zillah Forsyth began to rock herself to and fro. "Oh Lordy!" she chuckled. "Oh Lordy, Lordy! Why I've been engaged four times just this past year!" In a sudden passion of fastidiousness she bent down over the particular photograph in her hand and snatching at a handkerchief began to rub diligently at a small smouch of dust in one corner of the cardboard. Something in the effort of rubbing seemed to jerk her small round chin into almost angular prominence. "And before I'm through," she added, at least two notes below her usual alto tones, "And before I'm through - I'm going to get engaged to - every profession that there is on the surface of the globe!" Quite helplessly the thin paper skin of the photograph peeled off in company with the smouch of dust. "And when I marry," she ejaculated fiercely, "and when I marry - I'm going to marry a man who will take me to every place that there is - on the surface of the globe! And after that - !"

"After what?" interrogated a brand new voice from the doorway.

CHAPTER II

It was the other room-mate this time. The only real aristocrat in the whole graduating class, high-browed, high-cheekboned, - eyes like some far-sighted young prophet, - mouth even yet faintly arrogant with the ineradicable consciousness of caste, - a plain, eager, stripped-for-a-long-journey type of face, - this was Helene Churchill. There was certainly no innocuous bloom of country hills and pastures in this girl's face, nor any seething small-town passion pounding indiscriminately at all the doors of experience. The men and women who had bred Helene Churchill had been the breeders also of brick and granite cities since the world was new.

Like one infinitely more accustomed to treading on Persian carpets than on painted floors she came forward into the room.

"Hello, children!" she said casually, and began at once without further parleying to take down the motto that graced her own bureau-top.

It was the era when almost everybody in the world had a motto over his bureau. Helene Churchill's motto was: *Inasmuch As Ye Have Done It Unto One Of The Least Of These Ye Have Done It Unto Me.* On a scroll of almost priceless parchment the text was illuminated with inimitable Florentine skill and color. A little carelessly, after the manner of people quite accustomed to priceless things, she proceeded now to roll the parchment into its smallest possible circumference, humming exclusively to herself all the while an intricate little air from an Italian opera.

So the three faces foiled each other, sober city girl, pert town girl, bucolic country girl, - a hundred fundamental differences rampant between them, yet each fervid, adolescent young mouth tamed to the same monotonous, drolly exaggerated expression of complacency that characterizes the faces of all people who, in a distinctive uniform, for a reasonably satisfactory living wage, make an actual profession of righteous deeds.

Indeed among all the thirty or more varieties of noble expression which an indomitable Superintendent had finally succeeded in inculcating into her graduating class, no other physiognomies had responded more plastically perhaps than these three to the merciless imprint of the great *hospital machine* which, in pursuance of its one repetitive design, *discipline*, had coaxed Zillah Forsyth into the semblance of a lady, snubbed Helene Churchill into the substance of plain womanhood, and, still uncertain just what to do with Rae Malgregor's rollicking rural immaturity, had frozen her face temporarily into the smugly dimpled likeness of a fancy French doll rigged out as a nurse for some gilt-edged hospital fair.

With characteristic desire to keep up in every way with her more mature, better educated classmates, to do everything, in fact, so fast, so well, that no one should possibly guess that she hadn't yet figured out just why she was doing it at all, Rae Malgregor now with quickly readjusted cap and collar began to hurl herself into the task of her own packing. From her open bureau drawer, with a sudden impish impulse towards worldly wisdom, she extracted first of all the photograph of the young brakeman.

"See, Helene! My new beau!" she giggled experimentally.

In mild-eyed surprise Helene Churchill glanced up from her work. "*Your* beau?" she corrected. "Why, that's Zillah's picture."

"Well, it's mine now!" snapped Rae Malgregor with

unexpected edginess. "It's mine now all right. Zillah said I could have him! Zillah said I could - write to him - if I wanted to!" she finished a bit breathlessly.

Wider and wider Helene Churchill's eyes dilated. "Write to a man - whom you don't know?" she gasped. "Why, Rae! Why, it isn't even - very nice - to have a picture of a man you don't know!"

Mockingly to the edge of her strong white teeth Rae Malgregor's tongue crept out in pink derision. "Bah!" she taunted. "What's 'nice'? That's the whole matter with you, Helene Churchill! You never stop to consider whether anything's fun or not; all you care is whether it's 'nice'!" Excitedly she turned to meet the cheap little wink from Zillah's sainted eyes. "Bah! What's 'nice'?" she persisted a little lamely. Then suddenly all the pertness within her crumbled into nothingness. "That's - the - whole trouble with you, Zillah Forsyth!" she stammered. "You never give a hang whether anything's nice or not; all you care is whether it's fun!" Quite helplessly she began to wring her hands. "Oh, how do I know which one of you girls to follow?" she demanded wildly. "How do I know anything? How does anybody know anything?"

Like a smoldering fuse the rambling query crept back into the inner recesses of her brain and fired once more the one great question that lay dormant there. Impetuously she ran forward and stared into Helene Churchill's face. "How do you know you were meant to be a Trained Nurse, Helene Churchill?" she began all over again. "How does anybody know she was really meant to be one? How can anybody, I mean, be perfectly sure?" Like a drowning man clutching out at the proverbial straw, she clutched at the parchment in Helene Churchill's hand. "I mean - where did you get your motto, Helene Churchill?" she persisted with increasing irritability. "If - you don't tell me - I'll tear the whole thing to pieces!"

With a startled frown Helene Churchill jerked back out of

reach. "What's the matter with you, Rae?" she quizzed sharply, and then turning round quite casually to her book-case began to draw from the shelves one by one her beloved Marcus Aurelius, Wordsworth, Robert Browning. "Oh, I did so want to go to China," she confided irrelevantly. "But my family have just written me that they won't stand for it. So I suppose I'll have to go into tenement work here in the city instead." With a visible effort she jerked her mind back again to the feverish question in Rae Malgregor's eyes. "Oh, you want to know where I got my motto?" she asked. A flash of intuition brightened suddenly across her absent-mindedness. "Oh!" she smiled, "you mean you want to know - just what the incident was that first made me decide to - devote my life to - to humanity?"

"Yes!" snapped Rae Malgregor.

A little shyly Helene Churchill picked up her copy of Marcus Aurelius and cuddled her cheek against its tender Morocco cover. "Really?" she questioned with palpable hesitation. "Really you want to know? Why, why - it's rather a - sacred little story to me. I wouldn't exactly want to have anybody - laugh about it."

"I'll laugh if I want to!" attested Zillah Forsyth forcibly from the other side of the room.

Like a pugnacious boy, Rae Malgregor's fluent fingers doubled up into two firm fists.

"I'll punch her if she even looks as though she wanted to!" she signaled surreptitiously to Helene.

Shrewdly for an instant the city girl's narrowing eyes challenged and appraised the country girl's desperate sincerity. Then quite abruptly she began her little story.

"Why, it was on an Easter Sunday - Oh, ages and ages ago," she faltered. "Why, I couldn't have been more than nine years old at the time." A trifle self-consciously she turned her face away from Zillah Forsyth's supercilious smile. "And I was coming home from a Sunday school festival in my best white muslin dress with a big pot of purple pansies in my hand," she hastened somewhat nervously to explain. "And just at the edge of the gutter there was a dreadful drunken man lying in the mud with a great crowd of cruel people teasing and tormenting him. And, because - because I couldn't think of anything else to do about it, I - I walked right up to the poor old creature, - scared as I could be - and - and I presented him with my pot of purple pansies. And everybody of course began to laugh, to scream, I mean, and shout with amusement. And I, of course, began to cry. And the old drunken man straightened up very oddly for an instant, with his battered hat in one hand and the pot of pansies in the other, - and he raised the pot of pansies very high, as though it had been a glass of rarest wine - and bowed to me as - reverently as though he had been toasting me at my father's table at some very grand dinner. And 'Inasmuch!' he said. Just that, - 'Inasmuch!' So that's how I happened to go into nursing!" she finished as abruptly as she had begun. Like some wonderful phosphorescent manifestation her whole shining soul seemed to flare forth suddenly through her plain face.

With honest perplexity Zillah Forsyth looked up from her work.

"So that's - how you happened to go into nursing?" she quizzed impatiently. Her long, straight nose was all puckered tight with interrogation. Her dove-like eyes were fairly dilated with slow-dawning astonishment. "You - don't - mean?" she gasped. "You don't mean that - just for that - ?" Incredulously she jumped to her feet and stood staring blankly into the city girl's strangely illuminated features.

"Well, if I were a swell - like you!" she scoffed, "it would take a heap sight more than a drunken man munching pansies and rum and Bible-texts to - to jolt me out of my limousines and steam yachts and Adirondack bungalows!"

Quite against all intention Helene Churchill laughed. She did not often laugh. Just for an instant her eyes and Zillah Forsyth's clashed together in the irremediable antagonism of caste, - the Plebeian's scornful impatience with the Aristocrat, equaled only by the Aristocrat's condescending patience with the Plebeian.

It was no more than right that the Aristocrat should recover her self-possession first. "Never mind about your understanding. Zillah dear," she said softly. "Your hair is the most beautiful thing I ever saw in my life!"

Along Zillah Forsyth's ivory cheek an incongruous little flush of red began to show. With much more nonchalance than was really necessary she pointed towards her half-packed trunk.

"It wasn't - Sunday school - I was coming home from - when I got my motto!" she remarked dryly, with a wink at no one in particular. "And, so far as I know," she proceeded with increasing sarcasm, "the man who inspired my noble life was not in any way - particularly addicted to the use of alcoholic beverages!" As though her collar was suddenly too tight she rammed her finger down between her stiff white neck-band and her soft white throat. "He was a - New York doctor!" she hastened somewhat airily to explain. "Gee! But he was a swell! And he was spending his summer holiday up in the same Maine town where I was tending soda fountain. And he used to drop into the drug-store, nights, after cigars and things. And he used to tell me stories about the drugs and things, sitting up there on the counter swinging his legs and pointing out this and that, - quinine, ipecac, opium, hasheesh, - all the silly patent medicines, every sloppy soothing syrup! Lordy! He knew 'em as though they were people! Where they come from! Where they're going to! Yarns about the tropics that would kink the hair along the nape of your neck! Jokes about your own town's soup-kettle pharmacology that would make you yell for joy! Gee! But the things that man had seen and known! Gee! But the things that man could make you see and know! And he had an automobile," she confided proudly. "It was one of those billion dollar French cars. And I lived just round the corner from the drug-store. But we used to ride home by way of - New Hampshire!"

Almost imperceptibly her breath began to quicken. "Gee! Those nights!" she muttered. "Rain or shine, moon or thunder, - tearing down those country roads at forty miles an hour, singing, hollering, whispering! It was him that taught me to do my hair like this - instead of all the cheap rats and pompadours every other kid in town was wearing," she asserted, quite irrelevantly; then stopped with a quick, furtive glance of suspicion towards both her listeners and mouthed her way delicately back to the beginning of her sentence again. "It was *he* that taught me to do my hair like this," she repeated with the faintest possible suggestion of hauteur.

For one reason or another along the exquisitely chaste curve of her cheek a narrow streak of red began to show again.

"And he went away very sudden at the last," she finished hurriedly. "It seems he was married all the time." Blandly she turned her wonderful face to the caressing light. "And - I hope he goes to Hell!" she added perfectly simply.

With a little gasp of astonishment, shock, suspicion, distaste, Helene Churchill reached out an immediate conscientious hand to her.

"Oh, Zillah!" she began. "Oh, poor Zillah dear! I'm so - sorry! I'm so -"

Absolutely serenely, through a mask of insolence and ice, Zillah Forsyth ignored the proffered hand.

"I don't know what particular call you've got to be sorry for me, Helene Churchill," she drawled languidly. "I've got my character, same as you've got yours. And just about nine times as many good looks. And when it comes to nursing -" Like an alto song pierced suddenly by one shrill treble note, the girl's immobile face sharpened transiently with a single jagged flash of emotion. "And when it comes to nursing? Ha! Helene Churchill! You can lead your class all you want to with your silk-lined manners and your fuddy-duddy book-talk! But when genteel people like you are moping round all ready to fold your patients' hands on their breasts and murmur 'Thy will be done,' - why, that's the time that little 'yours truly' is just beginning to roll up her sleeves and get to work!"

With real passion her slender fingers went clutching again at her harsh linen collar. "It isn't you, Helene Churchill," she taunted, "that's ever been to the Superintendent on your bended knees and begged for the rabies cases - and the small-pox! Gee! You like nursing because you think it's pious to like it! But I like it - *because I like it!"* From brow to chin as though fairly stricken with sincerity her whole bland face furrowed startlingly with crude expressiveness. "The smell of ether!" she stammered. "It's like wine to me! The clang of the ambulance gong? I'd rather hear it than fire-engines! I'd crawl on my hands and knees a hundred miles to watch a major operation! I wish there was a war! I'd give my life to see a cholera epidemic!"

Abruptly as it came the passion faded from her face, leaving every feature tranquil again, demure, exaggeratedly innocent. With saccharine sweetness she turned to Rae Malgregor.

"Now, Little One," she mocked, "tell us the story of your lovely life. Having heard me coyly confess that I went into nursing because I had such a crush on this world, - and Helene here brazenly affirm that she went into nursing because she had such a crush on the world to come, - it's up to you now to confide to us just how you happened to take up so noble an endeavor! Had you seen some of the young house doctors' beautiful, smiling faces depicted in the hospital catalogue? Or was it for the sake of the Senior Surgeon's grim, gray mug that you jilted your poor plow-boy lover way up in the Annapolis Valley?"

"Why, Zillah!" gasped the country girl. "Why, I think you 're perfectly awful! Why, Zillah Forsyth! Don't you ever say a thing like that again! You can joke all you want to about the flirty young Internes. They're nothing but fellows. But it isn't - it isn't respectful - for you to talk like that about the Senior Surgeon. He's too - too terrifying!" she finished in an utter panic of consternation.

"Oh, now I know it was the Senior Surgeon that made you jilt your country beau!" taunted Zillah Forsyth with soft alto sarcasm.

"I didn't, either, jilt Joe Hazeltine!" stormed Rae Malgregor explosively. Backed up against her bureau, eyes flaming, breast heaving, little candy-box cap all tossed askew over her left ear, she stood defying her tormentor. "I didn't, either, jilt Joe Hazeltine!" she reasserted passionately. "It was Joe Hazeltine that jilted me! And we 'd been going together since we were kids! And now he's married the dominie's daughter and they've got a kid of their own most as old as he and I were when we first began courting each other. And it's all because I insisted on being a trained nurse," she finished shrilly.

With an expression of real shock Helene Churchill peered up from her lowly seat on the floor.

"You mean?" she asked a bit breathlessly. "You mean that he didn't want you to be a trained nurse? You mean that he wasn't big enough, - wasn't fine enough to appreciate the nobility of the profession?"

"Nobility nothing!" snapped Rae Malgregor. "It was me scrubbing strangemen with alcohol that he couldn't stand for! And I don't know as I exactly blame him," she added huskily. "It certainly is a good deal of a liberty when you stop to think about it."

Quite incongruously her big, childish, blue eyes narrowed suddenly into two dark, calculating slits. "It's comic," she mused, "how there isn't a man in the world who would stand letting his wife or daughter or sister have a male nurse. But look at the jobs we girls get sent out on! It's very confusing!"

With sincere appeal she turned to Zillah Forsyth. "And yet - and yet," she stammered. "And yet - when everything scary that's in you has once been scared out of you, - why, there's nothing left in you to be scared *with* any more, is there?"

"What? What?" pleaded Helene Churchill. "Say it again! What?"

"That's what Joe and I quarreled about my first vacation home!" persisted Rae Malgregor. "It was a traveling salesman's thigh. It was broken bad. Somebody had to take care of it. So I did! Joe thought it wasn't modest to be so willing." With a perplexed sort of defiance she raised her square little chin. "But you see I was willing!" she said. "I was perfectly willing. Just one single solitary year of hospital training had made me perfectly willing. And you can't *un*-willing a willing - even to please your beau, no matter how hard you try!" With a droll admixture of shyness and disdain she tossed her curly blonde head a trifle higher. "Shucks!" she attested. "What's a traveling salesman's thigh?"

"Shucks yourself!" scoffed Zillah Forsyth. "What's a silly beau or two up in Nova Scotia to a girl with looks like you? You could have married that typhoid case a dozen times last winter if you'd crooked your little finger! Why, the fellow was crazy about you. And he was richer than Croesus. What queered it?" she demanded bluntly. "Did his mother hate you?"

Like one fairly cramped with astonishment Rae Malgregor doubled up very suddenly at the waist-line, and thrusting her neck oddly forward after the manner of a startled crane, stood peering sharply round the corner of the rocking-chair at Zillah Forsyth.

"Did his mother hate me?" she gasped. "Did - his - mother -

hate - me? Well, what do you think? With me who never even saw plumbing till I came down here, setting out to explain to her with twenty tiled bathrooms how to be hygienic though rich? Did his mother hate me? Well, what do you think? With her who bore him, her who *bore* him, mind you, kept waiting down stairs in the hospital ante-room - half an hour every day - on the raw edge of a rattan chair - waiting - worrying - all old and gray and scared - while little young, perky, pink and white *me* is upstairs - brushing her own son's hair and washing her own son's face - and altogether getting her own son ready to see his own mother! And then me obliged to turn her out again in ten minutes, flip as you please, for fear she'd stayed too long, - while I stay on the rest of the night? *Did his mother hate me!"*

Stealthily as an assassin she crept around the corner of the rocking-chair and grabbed Zillah Forsyth by her astonished linen shoulder.

"Did his mother hate me?" she persisted mockingly. "Did his mother hate me? Well rather! Is there any woman from here to Kamchatka who doesn't hate us? Is there any woman from here to Kamchatka who doesn't look upon a trained nurse as her natural born enemy? I don't blame 'em!" she added chokingly. "Look at the impudent jobs we get sent out on! Quarantined upstairs for weeks at a time with their inflammable, diphtheritic bridegrooms - while they sit down stairs - brooding over their wedding teaspoons! Hiked off indefinitely to Atlantic City with their gouty bachelor uncles! Hearing their own innocent little sisters' blood-curdling deathbed deliriums! Snatching their own new-born babies away from their breasts and showing them, virgin-handed, how to nurse them better! The impudence of it, I say! The disgusting, confounded impudence! Doing things perfectly - flippantly - *right* - for twenty-five dollars a week - and washing - that all the achin' love in the world don't know how to do right - just for love!"

Furiously she began to jerk her victim's shoulder. "I tell you it's awful, Zillah Forsyth!" she insisted. "I tell you I just won't stand it!"

With muscles like steel wire Zillah Forsyth scrambled to her feet, and pushed Rae Malgregor back against the bureau.

"For Heaven's sake, Rae, shut up!" she said. "What in Creation's the matter with you to-day? I never saw you act so before!" With real concern she stared into the girl's turbid eyes. "If you feel like that about it, what in thunder did you go into nursing for?" she demanded not unkindly.

Very slowly Helene Churchill rose from her lowly seat by her precious book-case and came round and looked at Rae Malgregor rather oddly. "Yes," faltered Helene Churchill. "What did you go into nursing for?" The faintest possible taint of asperity was in her voice.

Quite dumbly for an instant Rae Malgregor's natural timidity stood battling the almost fanatic professional fervor in Helene Churchill's frankly open face, the raw, scientific passion, of very different caliber, but no less intensity, hidden so craftily behind Zillah Forsyth's plastic features. Then suddenly her own hands went clutching back at the bureau for support, and all the flaming, raging red went ebbing out of her cheeks, leaving her lips with hardly blood enough left to work them.

"I went into nursing," she mumbled, "and it's God's own truth, - I went into nursing because - because I thought the uniforms were so cute."

Furiously, the instant the words were gone from her mouth, she turned and snarled at Zillah's hooting laughter.

"Well, I had to do something!" she attested. The defense was like a flat blade slapping the air.

Desperately she turned to Helene Churchill's goading, faintly supercilious smile, and her voice edged suddenly like a twisted sword. "Well, the uniforms *are* cute!" she parried. "They are! They are! I bet you there's more than one girl standing high in the graduating class to-day who never would have stuck out her first year's bossin' and slops and worry and death - if she'd had to stick it out in the unimportant looking clothes she came from home in! Even you, Helene Churchill, with all your pious talk, - the day they put your coachman's son in as new Interne and you got called down from the office for failing to stand when Mr. Young Coachman came into the room, you bawled all night, - you did, - and swore you'd chuck your whole job and go home the next day - if it wasn't that you'd just had a life-size photo taken in full nursing costume to send to your brother's chum at Yale! So there!"

With a gasp of ineffable satisfaction she turned from Helene Churchill.

"Sure the uniforms are cute!" she slashed back at Zillah Forsyth. "That's the whole trouble with 'em. They're so awfully - masqueradishly - cute! Sure, I could have got engaged to the Typhoid Boy. It would have been as easy as robbing a babe! But lots of girls, I notice, get engaged in their uniforms, feeding a patient perfectly scientifically out of his own silver spoon, who don't seem to stay engaged so especially long in their own street clothes, bungling just plain naturally with their own knives and forks! Even you, Zillah Forsyth," she hacked, "even you who trot round like the Lord's Anointed in your pure white togs, you're just as Dutchy looking as anybody else, come to put you in a red hat and a tan coat and a blue skirt!"

Mechanically she raised her hands to her head as though with some silly thought of keeping the horrid pain in her temples from slipping to her throat, her breast, her feet.

"Sure the uniforms are cute," she persisted a bit thickly. "Sure the Typhoid Boy was crazy about me! He called me his 'Holy Chorus Girl,' I heard him - raving in his sleep. Lord save us! What are we to any man but just that?" she questioned hotly with renewed venom. "Parson, actor, young sinner, old saint - I ask you frankly, girls, on your word of honor, was there ever more than one man in ten went through your hands who didn't turn out soft somewhere before you were through with him? Mawking about your 'sweet eyes' while you're wrecking your optic nerves trying to decipher the dose on a poison bottle! Mooning over your wonderful likeness to the lovely young sister they - never had! Trying to kiss your finger tips when you're struggling to brush their teeth! Teasin' you to smoke cigarettes with 'em - when they know it would cost you your job!"

Impishly, without any warning, she crooked her knee and pointed at one homely square-toed shoe in a mincy dancing step. Hoydenishly she threw out her arms and tried to gather Helene and Zillah both into their compass.

"Oh, you Holy Chorus Girls!" she chuckled with maniacal delight. "Everybody, all together, now! Kick your little kicks! Smile your little smiles! Tinkle your little thermometers! Steady, - there! One - two - three - One - two - three!"

Laughingly Zillah Forsyth slipped from the grasp. "Don't you dare 'holy' me!" she threatened.

In real irritation Helene released herself. "I'm no chorus girl," she said coldly.

With a little shrill scream of pain Rae Malgregor's hands went flying back to her temples. Like a person giving orders in a great panic she turned authoritatively to her two room-mates, her fingers all the while boring frenziedly into her temples.

"Now, girls," she warned, "stand well back! If my head bursts, you know, it's going to burst all to slivers and splinters - like a boiler!"

"Rae, you're crazy!" hooted Zillah.

"Just plain vulgar - looney," faltered Helene.

Both girls reached out simultaneously to push her aside.

Somewhere in the dusty, indifferent street a bird's note rang out in one wild, delirious ecstasy of untrammeled springtime. To all intents and purposes the sound might have been the one final signal that Rae Malgregor's jangled nerves were waiting for.

"Oh, I *am* crazy, am I?" she cried with a new, fierce joy. "Oh, I *am* crazy, am I? Well, I'll go ask the Superintendent and see if I am! Oh, surely they wouldn't try and make me graduate if I really was crazy!"

Madly she bolted for her bureau, and snatching her own motto down, crumpled its face securely against her skirt and started for the door. Just what the motto was no one but herself knew. Sprawling in paint-brush hieroglyphics on a great flapping sheet of brown wrapping-paper, the sentiment, whatever it was, had been nailed face down to the wall for three tantalizing years.

"No you don't!" cried Zillah now, as she saw the mystery threatening so meanly to escape her.

"No you don't!" cried Helene. "You've seen our mottoes - and now we're going to see yours!"

Almost crazed with new terror Rae Malgregor went dodging to the right, - to the left, - to the right again, - cleared the rocking-chair, - a scuffle with padded hands, - climbed the trunk, - a race with padded feet, - reached the door-handle at last, yanked the door open, and with lungs and temper fairly bursting with momentum, shot down the hall, - down some stairs, - down some more hall, - down some more stairs, to the Superintendent's office where, with her precious motto still clutched securely in one hand, she broke upon that dignitary's startled, near-sighted vision like a young whirl-wind of linen and starch and flapping brown paper. Breathlessly, without prelude or preamble, she hurled her grievance into the older woman's grievance-dulled ears.

"Give me back my own face!" she demanded peremptorily. "Give me back my own face, I say! And my own hands! I tell you I want my own hands! Helene and Zillah say I'm insane! And I want to go home!"

CHAPTER III

Like a short-necked animal elongated suddenly to the cervical proportions of a giraffe, the Superintendent of Nurses reared up from her stoop-shouldered desk-work and stared forth in speechless astonishment across the top of her spectacles.

Exuberantly impertinent, ecstatically self-conscious, Rae Malgregor repeated her demand. To her parched mouth the very taste of her own babbling impudence refreshed her like the shock and prickle of cracked ice.

"I tell you I want my own face again! And my own hands!" she reiterated glibly. "I mean the face with the mortgage in it, and the cinders - and the other human expressions!" she explained. "And the nice grubby country hands that go with that sort of a face!"

Very accusingly she raised her finger and shook it at the Superintendent's perfectly livid countenance.

"Oh, of course I know I wasn't very much to look at. But at least I matched! What my hands knew, I mean, my face knew! Pies or plowing or May-baskets, what my hands knew my face knew! That's the way hands and faces ought to work together! But you? you with all your rules and your bossing and your everlasting 'S - sh! S - sh!' you've snubbed all the know-anything out of my face - and made my hands nothing but two disconnected machines - for somebody else to run! And I hate you! You're a Monster! You're a - , everybody hates you!"

Mutely then she shut her eyes, bowed her head, and waited for the Superintendent to smite her dead. The smite she felt quite sure would be a noisy one. First of all, she reasoned it would fracture her skull. Naturally then of course it would splinter her spine. Later in all probability it would telescope her knee-joints. And never indeed now that she came to think of it had the arches of her feet felt less capable of resisting so terrible an impact. Quite unconsciously she groped out a little with one hand to steady herself against the edge of the desk.

But the blow when it came was nothing but a cool finger tapping her pulse.

"There! There!" crooned the Superintendent's voice with a most amazing tolerance.

"But I won't 'there - there'!" snapped Rae Malgregor. Her eyes were wide open again now, and extravagantly dilated.

The cool fingers on her pulse seemed to tighten a little. "S - sh! S - sh!" admonished the Superintendent's mumbling lips.

"But I won't 'S - sh - S - sh'!" stormed Rae Malgregor. Never before in her three years' hospital training had she seen her arch-enemy, the Superintendent, so utterly disarmed of irascible temper and arrogant dignity, and the sight perplexed and maddened her at one and the same moment. "But I won't 'S - sh - S - sh'!" Desperately she jerked her curly blonde head in the direction of the clock on the wall. "Here it's four o'clock now!" she cried. "And in less than four hours you're going to try and make me graduate - and go out into the world - God knows where - and charge innocent people twenty-five dollars a week and washing, likelier than not, mind you, for these hands," she gestured, "that don't co-ordinate at all with this face," she grimaced, "but with the face of one of the House Doctors - or the Senior Surgeon - or even you - who may be way off in Kamchatka - when I need him most!" she finished with a confused jumble of accusation and despair.

Still with unexplainable amiability the Superintendent whirled back into place in her pivot-chair and with her left hand which had all this time been rummaging busily in a lower desk drawer proffered Rae Malgregor a small fold of paper.

"Here, my dear," she said. "Here's a sedative for you. Take it at once. It will quiet you perfectly. We all know you've had very hard luck this past month, but you mustn't worry so about the future." The slightest possible tinge of purely professional manner crept back into the older woman's voice. "Certainly, Miss Malgregor, with your judgment -"

"With my judgment?" cried Rae Malgregor. The phrase was like a red rag to her. "With my judgment? Great Heavens! That's the whole trouble! I haven't got any judgment! I've never been allowed to have any judgment! All I've ever been allowed to have is the judgment of some flirty young medical student - or the House Doctor! - or the Senior Surgeon! - or you!"

Her eyes were fairly piteous with terror.

"Don't you see that my face doesn't know anything?" she faltered, "except just to smile and smile and smile and say 'Yes, sir - No, sir - Yes, sir'?" From curly blonde head to square-toed, commonsense shoes her little body began to quiver suddenly like the advent of a chill. "Oh, what am I going to do," she begged, "when I'm way off alone - somewhere - in the mountains - or a tenement - or a palace - and something happens - and there isn't any judgment round to tell me what I ought to do?"

Abruptly in the doorway as though summoned by some purely casual flicker of the Superintendent's thin fingers another nurse appeared.

"Yes, I rang," said the Superintendent. "Go and ask the Senior Surgeon if he can come to me here a moment, immediately."

"The Senior Surgeon?" gasped Rae Malgregor. "The Senior Surgeon?" With her hands clutching at her throat she reeled back against the wall for support. Like a shore bereft in one second of its tide, like a tree stripped in one second of its leafage, she stood there, utterly stricken of temper or passion or any animating human emotion whatsoever.

"Oh, now I'm going to be expelled! Oh, now I know I'm going to be - expelled!" she moaned listlessly.

Very vaguely into the farthest radiation of her vision she sensed the approach of a man. Gray-haired, gray-bearded, gray-suited, grayly dogmatic as a block of granite, the Senior Surgeon loomed up at last in the doorway.

"I'm in a hurry," he growled. "What's the matter?"

Precipitously Rae Malgregor collapsed into the breach.

"Oh, there's - nothing at all the matter, sir," she stammered. "It's only - it's only that I've just decided that I don't want to be a trained nurse."

With a gesture of ill-concealed impatience the Superintendent shrugged the absurd speech aside.

"Dr. Faber," she said, "won't you just please assure Miss Malgregor once more that the little Italian boy's death last week was in no conceivable way her fault, - that nobody blames her in the slightest, or holds her in any possible way responsible."

"Why, what nonsense!" snapped the Senior Surgeon. "What -!"

"And the Portuguese woman the week before that," interrupted Rae Malgregor dully.

"Stuff and nonsense!" said the Senior Surgeon. "It's nothing but coincidence! Pure coincidence! It might have happened to anybody!"

"And she hasn't slept for almost a fortnight." the Superintendent confided, "nor touched a drop of food or drink, as far as I can make out, except just black coffee. I've been expecting this break-down for some days."

"And-the-young-drug-store-clerk-the-week-before-that," Rae Malgregor resumed with sing-song monotony.

Brusquely the Senior Surgeon stepped forward and taking the girl by her shoulders, jerked her sharply round to the light, and, with firm, authoritative fingers, rolled one of her eyelids deftly back from its inordinately dilated pupil. Equally brusquely he turned away again.

"Nothing but moonshine!" he muttered. "Nothing in the world but too much coffee dope taken on an empty stomach, - 'empty brain,' I'd better have said! When will you girls ever learn any sense?" With searchlight shrewdness his eyes flashed back for an instant over the haggard gray lines that slashed along the corners of her quivering, childish mouth. A bit temperishly he began to put on his gloves. "Next time you set out to have a 'brain-storm,' Miss Malgregor," he suggested satirically, "try to have it about something more sensible than imagining that anybody is trying to hold you personally responsible for the existence of death in the world. Bah!" he ejaculated fiercely. "If you are going to fuss like this over cases hopelessly moribund from the start, what in thunder are you going to do some fine day when out of a perfectly clear and clean sky Security itself turns septic and you lose the President of the United States - or a mother of nine children - with a hang-nail?"

"But I wasn't fussing, sir!" protested Rae Malgregor with a timid sort of dignity. "Why, it never had occurred to me for a moment that anybody blamed me for - anything!" Just from sheer astonishment her hands took a new clutch into the torn flapping corner of the motto that she still clung desperately to even at this moment.

"For Heaven's sake stop crackling that brown paper!" stormed the Senior Surgeon.

"But I wasn't crackling the brown paper, sir! It's crackling itself," persisted Rae Malgregor very softly. The great blue eyes that lifted to his were brimming full of misery. "Oh, can't I make you understand, sir?" she stammered. Appealingly she turned to the Superintendent. "Oh, can't I make anybody understand? All I was trying to say, - all I was trying to explain, was - that I *don't want to be a trained nurse – after all*!"

"Why not?" demanded the Senior Surgeon with a rather noisy click of his glove fasteners.

"Because - my - face - is - tired," said the girl quite simply.

The explosive wrath on the Senior Surgeon's countenance seemed to be directed suddenly at the Superintendent.

"Is this an afternoon tea?" he asked tartly. "With six major operations this morning and a probable meningitis diagnosis ahead of me this afternoon I think I might be spared the babblings of an hysterical nurse!" Casually over his shoulder he nodded at the girl. "You're a fool!" he said, and started for the door.

Just on the threshold he turned abruptly and looked back. His forehead was furrowed like a corduroy road and the one rampant question in his mind at the moment seemed to be mired hopelessly between his bushy eyebrows.

"Lord!" he exclaimed a bit flounderingly. "Are *you* the nurse that helped me last week on that fractured skull?"

"Yes, sir," said Rae Malgregor.

Jerkily the Senior Surgeon retraced his footsteps into the office and stood facing her as though with some really terrible accusation.

"And the freak abdominal?" he quizzed sharply. "Was it *you* who threaded that needle for me so blamed slowly - and calmly - and surely, while all the rest of us were jumping up and down and cursing you - for no brighter reason than that we couldn't have threaded it ourselves if we'd had all eternity before us and - all creation bleeding to death?"

"Y-e-s, sir," said Rae Malgregor.

Quite bluntly the Senior Surgeon reached out and lifted one of her hands to his scowling professional scrutiny.

"Gad!" he attested. "What a hand! You're a wonder! Under proper direction you're a wonder! It was like myself working with twenty fingers and no thumbs! I never saw anything like it!"

Almost boyishly the embarrassed flush mounted to his cheeks as he jerked away again. "Excuse me for not recognizing you," he apologized gruffly. "But you girls all look so much alike!"

As though the eloquence of Heaven itself had suddenly descended upon a person hitherto hopelessly tongue-tied, Rae Malgregor lifted an utterly transfigured face to the Senior Surgeon's grimly astonished gaze.

"Yes! Yes, sir!" she cried joyously. "That's just exactly what the trouble is! That's just exactly what I was trying to express, sir! My face is all worn out trying to 'look alike'! My cheeks are almost sprung with artificial smiles! My eyes are fairly bulging with unshed tears! My nose aches like a toothache trying never to turn up at anything! I'm smothered with the discipline of it! I'm choked with the affectation! I tell you - I just can't breathe through a trained nurse's face any more! I tell you, sir, I'm sick to death of being nothing but a type. I want to look like *myself!* I want to see what Life could do to a silly face like mine - if it ever got a chance! When other women are crying, I want the fun of crying! When other women look scared to death, I want the fun of looking scared to death!" Hysterically again with shrewish emphasis she began to repeat: "I won't be a nurse! I tell you, I won't! I *won't*!"

"Pray what brought you so suddenly to this remarkable decision?" scoffed the Senior Surgeon.

"A letter from my father, sir," she confided more quietly. "A letter about some dogs."

"Dogs?" hooted the Senior Surgeon.

"Yes, sir," said the White Linen Nurse. A trifle speculatively for an instant she glanced at the Superintendent's face and then back again to the Senior Surgeon's. "Yes, sir," she repeated with increasing confidence. "Up in Nova Scotia my father raises hunting-dogs. Oh, no special fancy kind, sir," she hastened in all honesty to explain. "Just dogs, you know, - just mixed dogs, - pointers with curly tails, - and shaggy-coated hounds, - and brindled spaniels, and all that sort of thing, - just mongrels, you know, but very clever; and people, sir, come all the way from Boston to buy dogs of him, and once a man came way from London to learn the secret of his training."

"Well, what is the secret of his training?" quizzed the Senior Surgeon with the sudden eager interest of a sportsman. "I should think it would be pretty hard," he acknowledged, "in a mixed gang like that to decide just which particular dog was suited to what particular game!"

"Yes, that's just it, sir," beamed the White Linen Nurse. "A dog, of course, will chase anything that runs, - that's just dog, - but when a dog really begins to *care* for what he's chasing he - wags! That's hunting! Father doesn't calculate, he says, on training a dog on anything he doesn't wag on!"

"Yes, but what's that got to do with you?" asked the Senior

Surgeon a bit impatiently.

With ill-concealed dismay the White Linen Nurse stood staring blankly at the Senior Surgeon's gross stupidity.

"Why, don't you see?" she faltered. "I've been chasing this nursing job three whole years now - and there's no wag to it!"

"Oh Hell!" said the Senior Surgeon. If he hadn't said "Oh Hell!" he would have grinned. And it hadn't been a grinning day, and he certainly didn't intend to begin grinning at any such late hour as that in the afternoon. With his dignity once reassured he relaxed then a trifle. "For Heaven's sake, what *do* you want to be?" he asked not unkindly.

With an abrupt effort at self-control Rae Malgregor jerked her head into at least the outer semblance of a person lost in almost fathomless thought.

"Why I'm sure I don't know, sir," she acknowledged worriedly. "But it would be a great pity, I suppose, to waste all the grand training that's gone into my hands." With sudden conviction her limp shoulders stiffened a trifle. "My oldest sister," she stammered, "bosses the laundry in one of the big hotels in Halifax, and my youngest sister teaches school in Moncton. But I'm so strong, you know, and I like to move things round so, - and everything, - maybe - I could get a position somewhere as general housework girl."

With a roar of amusement as astonishing to himself as to his listeners, the Senior Surgeon's chin jerked suddenly upward.

"You're crazy as a loon!" he confided cordially. "Great Scott! If you can work up a condition like this on coffee, - what would you do on," he hesitated grimly, "malted milk?" As unheralded as his amusement, gross irritability overtook him again. "Will - you - stop - rattling that brown paper?" he thundered at her.

Innocently as a child she rebuffed the accusation and ignored the temper.

"But I'm not rattling it, sir!" she protested. "I'm simply trying to hide what's on the other side of it."

"What is on the other side of it?" demanded the Senior Surgeon bluntly.

With unquestioning docility the girl turned the paper around.

From behind her desk the austere Superintendent twisted her neck most informally to decipher the scrawling hieroglyphics. "*Don't - Ever - Be - bumptious*!" she read forth jerkily with a questioning, incredulous sort of emphasis.

"Don't ever be bumptious?" squinted the Senior Surgeon perplexedly through his glasses.

"Yes," said Rae Malgregor very timidly. "It's my - motto."

"Your motto?" sniffed the Superintendent.

"Your motto?" chuckled the Senior Surgeon.

"Yes, my motto," repeated Rae Malgregor with the slightest perceptible tinge of resentment. "And it's a perfectly good motto, too! Only, of course, it hasn't got any style to it. That's why I didn't want the girls to see it," she confided a bit drearily. Then palpably before their eyes they saw her spirit leap into ineffable pride. "My Father gave it to me," she announced briskly. "And my Father said that, when I came home in June, if I could honestly say that I'd never once been bumptious - all my three years here, - he'd give me a - heifer! And -"

"Well I guess you've lost your heifer!" said the Senior Surgeon bluntly.

"Lost my heifer?" gasped the girl. Big-eyed and incredulous she stood for an instant staring back and forth from the Superintendent's face to the Senior Surgeon's. "You mean?" she stammered, "you mean - that I've - been - bumptious - just now? You mean - that after all these years of - meachin' meekness - I've lost - ?"

Plainly even to the Senior Surgeon and the Superintendent the bones in her knees weakened suddenly like knots of tissue paper. No power on earth could have made her break discipline by taking a chair while the Senior Surgeon stood, so she sank limply down to the floor instead, with two great solemn tears welling slowly through the fingers with which she tried vainly to cover her face.

"And the heifer was brown, with one white ear; it was awful cunning," she confided mumblingly. "And it ate from my hand - all warm and sticky, like - loving sandpaper." There was no protest in her voice, nor any whine of complaint, but merely the abject submission to Fate of one who from earliest infancy had seen other crops blighted by other frosts. Then tremulously with the air of one who, just as a matter of spiritual tidiness, would purge her soul of all sad secrets, she lifted her entrancing, tear-flushed face from her strong, sturdy, utterly unemotional fingers and stared with amazing blueness, amazing blandness into the Senior Surgeon's scowling scrutiny.

"And I'd named her - for you!" she said. "I'd named her - Patience - for you!"

Instantly then she scrambled to her knees to try and assuage by somemiraculous apology the horrible shock which she read in the Senior Surgeon's face.

"Oh, of course, sir, I know it isn't scientific!" she pleaded desperately. "Oh, of course, sir, I know it isn't scientific at all! But up where I live, you know, instead of praying for anybody, we - we name a young animal - for the virtue that that person - seems to need the most. And if you tend the young animal carefully - and train it right - ! Why - it's just a superstition, of course, but - Oh, sir!" she floundered hopelessly, "the virtue you needed most in your business was what I meant! Oh, really, sir, I never thought of criticizing your character!"

Gruffly the Senior Surgeon laughed. Embarrassment was in the laugh, and anger, and a fierce, fiery sort of resentment against both the embarrassment and the anger, - but no possible trace of amusement. Impatiently he glanced up at the fast speeding clock.

"Good Lord!" he exclaimed, "I'm an hour late now!" Scowling like a pirate he clicked the cover of his watch open and shut for an uncertain instant. Then suddenly he laughed again, and there was nothing whatsoever in his laugh this time except just amusement.

"See here, Miss - Bossy Tamer," he said. "If the Superintendent is willing, go get your hat and coat, and I'll take you out on that meningitis case with me. It's a thirty mile run if it's a block, and I guess if you sit on the front seat it will blow the cobwebs out of your brain - if anything will," he finished not unkindly.

Like a white hen sensing the approach of some utterly unseen danger the Superintendent seemed to bristle suddenly in every direction.

"It's a bit - irregular," she protested in her most even tone.

"Bah! So are some of the most useful of the French verbs!" snapped the Senior Surgeon. In the midst of authority his voice could be inestimably soft and reassuring, but sometimes on the brink of asserting said authority he had a tone that was distinctly unpleasant.

"Oh, very well," conceded the Superintendent with some waspishness.

Hazily for an instant Rae Malgregor stood staring into the

Superintendent's uncordial face. "I'd - I'd apologize," she faltered, "but I - don't even know what I said. It just blew up!"

Perfectly coldly and perfectly civilly the Superintendent received the overture. "It was quite evident, Miss Malgregor, that you were not altogether responsible at the moment," she conceded in common justice.

Heavily then, like a person walking in her sleep the girl trailed out of the room to get her coat and hat.

Slamming one desk-drawer after another the Superintendent drowned the sluggish sound of her retreating footsteps.

"There goes my best nurse!" she said grimly. "My very best nurse! Oh no, not the most brilliant one, I didn't mean that, but the most reliable! The most nearly perfect human machine that it has ever been my privilege to see turned out, - the one girl that week in, week out, month after month, and year after year, has always done what she's told, - when she was told, - and the exact way she was told, - without questioning anything, without protesting anything, without supplementing anything with some disastrous original conviction of her own - *and look at her now*!" Tragically the Superintendent rubbed her hand across her worried brow. "Coffee, you said it was?" she asked skeptically. "Are there any special antidotes for coffee?"

With a queer little quirk to his mouth the gruff Senior Surgeon jerked his glance back from the open window where with the gleam of a slim torn-boyish ankle the frisky young Spring went scurrying through the tree-tops.

"What's that you asked?" he quizzed sharply. "Any antidotes for coffee? Yes. Dozens of them. But none for Spring."

"Spring?" sniffed the Superintendent. A little shiveringly she reached out and gathered a white knitted shawl around her shoulders. "Spring? I don't see what Spring's got to do with

Rae Malgregor or any other young outlaw in my graduating class. If graduation came in November it would be just the same! They're a set of ingrates, every one of them!" Vehemently she turned aside to her card-index of names and slapped the cards through one by one without finding one single soothing exception. "Yes, sir, a set of ingrates!" she repeated accusingly. "Spend your life trying to teach them what to do and how to do it! Cram ideas into those that haven't got any, and yank ideas out of those who have got too many! Refine them, toughen them, scold them, coax them, everlastingly drill and discipline them! And then, just as you get them to a place where they move like clock-work, and you actually believe you can trust them, then graduation day comes round, and they think they're all safe, - and every single individual member of the class breaks out and runs a-muck with the one dare-devil deed she's been itching to do every day the past three years! Why this very morning I caught the President of the Senior Class with a breakfast tray in her hands - stealing the cherry out of her patient's grape fruit. And three of the girls reported for duty as bold as brass with their hair frizzed tight as a nigger doll's. And the girl who's going into a convent next week was trying on the laundryman's derby hat as I came up from lunch. And now, now -" the Superintendent's voice went suddenly a little hoarse, "and now - here's Miss Malgregor - intriguing - to get an automobile ride with - *you!*"

"Eh?" cried the Senior Surgeon with a jump. "What? Is this an Insane Asylum? Is it a Nervine?" Madly he started for the door. "Order a ton of bromides!" he called back over his shoulder. "Order a car-load of them! Saturate the whole place with them! Drown the whole damned place!"

Half way down the lower hall, all his nerves on edge, all his unwonted boyish impulsiveness quenched noxiously like a candle flame, he met and passed Rae Malgregor without a sign of recognition.

"God! How I hate women!" he kept mumbling to himself as he

struggled clumsily all alone into the torn sleeve lining of his thousand dollar mink coat.

CHAPTER IV

Like a train-traveler coming out of a long, smoky, smothery tunnel Into the clean-tasting light, the White Linen Nurse came out of the prudish-smelling hospital into the riotous mud-and-posie promise of the young April afternoon.

The God of Hysteria had certainly not deserted her! In all the full effervescent reaction of her brain-storm, - fairly bubbling with dimples, fairly foaming with curls, - light-footed, light-hearted, most ecstatically light-headed, she tripped down into the sunshine as though the great, harsh, granite steps that marked her descent were nothing more nor less than a gigantic, old, horny-fingered hand passing her blithely out to some deliciously unknown Lilliputian adventure.

As she pranced across the soggy April sidewalk to what she supposed was the Senior Surgeon's perfectly empty automobile she became conscious suddenly that the rear seat of the car was already occupied.

Out from an unseasonable snuggle of sable furs and flaming red hair a small, peevish face peered forth at her with frank curiosity.

"Why, hello!" beamed the White Linen Nurse. "Who are you?"

With unmistakable hostility the haughty little face retreated into its furs and its red hair. "Hush!" commanded a shrill childish voice. "Hush, I say! I'm a cripple - and very bad-tempered. Don't speak to me!"

"Oh, my Glory!" gasped the White Linen Nurse. "Oh my Glory, Glory, Glory!" Without any warning whatsoever she felt suddenly like Nothing-At-All, rigged out in an exceedingly shabby old ulster and an excessively homely black slouch hat. In a desperate attempt at tangible tom-boyish nonchalance she tossed her head and thrust her hands down deep into her big ulster pockets. That the bleak hat reflected no decent featherish consciousness of being tossed, that the big threadbare pockets had no bottoms to them, merely completed her startled sense of having been in some way blotted right out of existence.

Behind her back the Senior Surgeon's huge fur-coated approach dawned blissfully like the thud of a rescue party.

But if the Senior Surgeon's blunt, wholesome invitation to ride had been perfectly sweet when he prescribed it for her in the Superintendent's office, the invitation had certainly soured most amazingly in the succeeding ten minutes. Abruptly now, without any greeting, he reached out and opened the rear door of the car, and nodded curtly for her to enter there.

Instantly across the face of the little crippled girl already ensconced in the tonneau a single flash of light went zig-zagging crookedly from brow to chin, - and was gone again. "Hello, Fat Father!" piped the shrill little voice. "Hello, - Fat Father!" Yet so subtly was the phrase mouthed, to save your soul you could not have proved just where the greeting ended and the taunt began.

There was nothing subtle however about the way in which the Senior Surgeon's hand shot out and slammed the tonneau door bang-bang again on its original passenger. His face was crimson with anger. Brusquely he pointed to the front seat.

"You may sit in there, with me, Miss Malgregor!" he thundered.

"Yes, sir," crooned the White Linen Nurse.

Meek as an oiled machine she scuttled to her appointed place. Once More in smothered giggle and unprotesting acquiescence she sensed the resumption of eternal discipline. Already in just this trice of time she felt her rampant young mouth resettle tamely into lines of smug, determinate serenity. Already across her idle lap she felt her clasped fingers begin to frost and tingle again like a cheerfully non-concerned bunch of live wires waiting the one authoritative signal to connect somebody, - anybody, - with this world or the next. Already the facile tip of her tongue seemed fairly loaded and cocked like a revolver with all the approximate "Yes, sirs," "No, sirs," that she thought she should probably need.

But the only immediate remarks that the Senior Surgeon addressed to any one were addressed distinctly to the crank of his automobile.

"Damn having a chauffeur who gets drunk the one day of the year when you need him most!" he muttered under his breath, as with the same exquisitely sensitive fingers that could have dissected like a caress the nervous system of a humming bird, or re-set unbruisingly the broken wing of a butterfly, he hurled his hundred and eighty pounds of infuriate brute-strength against the calm, chronic, mechanical stubbornness of that auto crank. "Damn!" he swore on the upward pull. "Damn!" he gasped on the downward push. "Damn!" he cursed and sputtered and spluttered. Purple with effort, bulging-eyed with strain, reeking with sweat, his frenzied outburst would have terrorized the entire hospital staff.

With an odd little twinge of homesickness, the White Linen Nurse slid cautiously out to the edge of her seat so that she might watch the struggle better. For thus, with dripping foreheads and knotted neck-muscles and breaking backs and rankly tempestuous language, did the untutored men-folk of her own beloved home-land hurl their great strength against bulls and boulders and refractory forest trees. Very startlingly as she watched, a brand new thought went zig-zagging through her consciousness. Was it possible, - was it even so much as remotely possible - that the great Senior Surgeon, - the great, wonderful, altogether formidable, altogether unapproachable Senior Surgeon, - was just a - was just a - ? Stripped ruthlessly of all his social superiority, - of all his professional halo, - of all his scientific achievement, the Senior Surgeon stood suddenly forth before her - a mere man - just like other men! *Just exactly* like other men? Like the sick drug-clerk? Like the new-born millionaire baby? Like the doddering old Dutch gaffer? The very delicacy of such a thought drove the blood panic-stricken from her face. It was the indelicacy of the thought that brought the blood surging back again to brow, to cheeks, to lips, even to the tips of her ears.

Glancing up casually from the roar and rumble of his abruptly repentant engine the Senior Surgeon swore once more under his breath to think that any female sitting perfectly idle and non-concerned in a seven thousand dollar car should have the nerve to flaunt such a furiously strenuous color.

Bristling with resentment and mink furs he strode around the fender and stumbled with increasing irritation across the White Linen Nurse's knees to his seat. Just for an instant his famous fingers seemed to flash with apparent inconsequence towards one bit of mechanism and another. Then like a huge, portentous pill floated on smoothest syrup the car slid down the yawning street into the congested city.

Altogether monotonously in terms of pain and dirt and drug and disease the city wafted itself in and out of the White Linen Nurse's well-grooved consciousness. From every filthy street corner sodden age or starved babyhood reached out its fluttering pulse to her. Then, suddenly sweet as a draught through a fever-tainted room, the squalid city freshened into jocund, luxuriant suburbs with rollicking tennis courts, and flaming yellow forsythia blossoms, and green velvet lawns prematurely posied with pale exotic hyacinths and great scarlet splotches of lusty tulips.

Beyond this hectic horticultural outburst the leisurely Spring faded out again into April's naturally sallow colors.

Glossy and black as an endless typewriter ribbon, the narrow, tense State Road seemed to wind itself everlastingly in - and in - and in - on some hidden spool of the car's mysterious mechanism. Clickety-Click-Click-Clack, - faster than any human mind could think, - faster than any human hand could finger, - hurtling up hazardous hills of thought, - sliding down facile valleys of fancy, - roaring with emphasis, - shrieking with punctuation, - the great car yielded itself perforce to Fate's dictation.

Robbed successively of the city's humanitarian pang, of the suburb's esthetic pleasure, the White Linen Nurse found herself precipitated suddenly into a mere blur of sight, a mere chaos of sound. In whizzing speed and crashing breeze, - houses - fences - meadows - people - slapped across her eyeballs like pictures on a fan. On and on and on through kaleidoscopic yellows and rushing grays the great car sped, a purely mechanical factor in a purely mechanical landscape.

Rigid with concentration the Senior Surgeon stared like a dead man into the intrepid, on-coming road.

Intermittently from her green, plushy laprobes the little crippled girl struggled to her feet, and sprawling clumsily across whose-ever shoulder suited her best, raised a brazenly innocent voice, deliberately flatted, in a shrill and maddeningly repetitive chant of her own making, to the effect that

All the birds were there
With yellow feathers instead of hair,
And bumble bees crocheted in the trees -
And bumble bees crocheted in the trees -

And all the birds were there -
And - And -

Intermittently from the front seat the Senior Surgeon's wooden face relaxed to the extent of a grim mouth twisting distractedly sideways in one furious bellow.

"Will - you - stop - your - *noise* - and - go - back - to - your - seat!"

Nothing else happened at all until at last, out of unbroken stretches of winter-staled stubble, a high, formal hemlock hedge and a neat, pebbled driveway proclaimed the Senior Surgeon's ultimate destination.

Cautiously now, with an almost tender skill, the big car circled a tiny, venturesome clump of highway violets and crept through a prancing, leaping fluff of yellow collie dogs to the door of the big stone house.

Instantly from inestimable resources a liveried serving man appeared to help the Surgeon from his car; another, to take the Surgeon's coat; another, to carry his bag.

Lingering for an instant to stretch his muscles and shake his great shoulders, the Senior Surgeon breathed into his cramped lungs a friendly impulse as well as a scent of budding cherry trees.

"You may come in with me, if you want to, Miss Malgregor." he conceded. "It's an extraordinary case. You will hardly see another one like it." Palpably he lowered his already almost indistinguishable voice. "The boy is young," he confided, "about your age, I should guess, a college foot-ball hero, the most superbly perfect specimen of young manhood it has ever been my privilege to behold. It will be a long case. They have two nurses already, but would like another. The work ought not to be hard. Now if they should happen to - fancy you!" In speechless expressiveness his eyes swept estimatingly over sun-parlors, stables, garages, Italian gardens, rapturous blue-shadowed mountain views - every last intimate detail of the mansion's wonderful equipment.

Like a drowning man feeling his last floating spar wrenched away from him, the White Linen Nurse dug her finger-nails frantically into every reachable wrinkle and crevice of the heavily upholstered seat.

"Oh, but sir, I don't want to go in!" she protested passionately. "I tell you, sir, I'm quite done with all that sort of thing! It would break my heart! It would! Oh, sir, this worrying about people for whom you've got no affection, - it's like sledding without any snow! It grits right down on your naked nerves. It -"

Before the Senior Surgeon's glowering, incredulous stare her heart began to plunge and pound again, but it plunged and pounded no harder, she realized suddenly, than when in the calm, white hospital precincts she was obliged to pass his terrifying presence in the corridor and murmur an inaudible "Good Morning" or "Good Evening." "After all, he's nothing but a man - nothing but a man - nothing but a mere - ordinary - two-legged man," she reasoned over and over to herself. With a really desperate effort she smoothed her frightened face into an expression of utter guilelessness and peace and smiled unflinchingly right into the Senior Surgeon's rousing anger as she had once seen an animal-trainer smile into the snarl of a crouching tiger.

"Th - ank you very much!" she said. "But I think I won't go in, sir, - thank you! My - my face is still pretty tired!"

"Idiot!" snapped the Senior Surgeon as he turned on his heel and started up the steps.

From the green plushy robes on the back seat the White Linen Nurse could have sworn that she heard a sharply ejaculated, maliciously joyful "Ha!" piped out. But when both she and the

Senior Surgeon turned sharply round to make sure, the Little Crippled Girl, in apparently complete absorption, sat amiably extracting tuft after tuft of fur from the thumb of one big sable glove, to the rumbling, sing-song monotone of "He loves me - Loves me not - Loves me - Loves me not."

Bristling with unutterable contempt for all femininity, the Senior Surgeon proceeded up the steps between two solemn-faced lackeys.

"Father!" wailed a feeble little voice. "Father!" There was no shrillness in the tone now, nor malice, nor any mischievous thing, - just desolation, the impulsive, panic-stricken desolation of a little child left suddenly alone with a stranger. "Father!" the frightened voice ventured forth a tiny bit louder. But the unheeding Senior Surgeon had already reached the piazza. "Fat Father!" screamed the little voice. Barbed now like a shark-hook the phrase ripped through the Senior Surgeon's dormant sensibilities. As one fairly yanked out of his thoughts he whirled around in his tracks.

"What do you want?" he thundered.

Helplessly the little girl sat staring from a lackey's ill-concealed grin to her Father's smoldering fury. Quite palpably she began to swallow with considerable difficulty. Then quick as a flash a diminutively crafty smile crooked across one corner of her mouth.

"Father?" she improvised dulcetly. "Father? May - may I - sit - in the White Linen Nurse's lap?"

Just for an instant the Senior Surgeon's narrowing eyes probed mercilessly into the reekingly false little smile. Then altogether brutally he shrugged his shoulders.

"I don't care where in blazes you sit!" he muttered, and went on into the house.

With an air of unalterable finality the massive oak door closed after him. In the resonant click of its latch the great wrought-iron lock seemed to smack its lips with ineffable satisfaction.

Wringing suddenly round with a whish of starched skirts the White Linen Nurse knelt up in her seat and grinned at the Little Crippled Girl.

"'Ha' - yourself!" she said.

Against all possible expectancy the Little Crippled Girl burst out laughing. The laugh was wild, ecstatic, extravagantly boisterous, yet awkward withal, and indescribably bumpy, like the first flight of a cage-cramped bird.

Quite abruptly the White Linen Nurse sat down again, and commenced nervously with the wrist of her chamois glove to polish the slightly tarnished brass lamp at her elbow. Equally abruptly after a minute she stopped polishing and looked back at the Little Crippled Girl.

"Would - you - like - to sit in my lap?" she queried conscientiously.

Insolent with astonishment the Little Girl parried the question. "Why in blazes - should I want to sit in your lap?" she quizzed harshly. Every accent of her voice, every remotest intonation, was like the Senior Surgeon's at his worst. The suddenly forked eyebrow, the snarling twitch of the upper lip, turned the whole delicate little face into a grotesque but desperately unconscious caricature of the grim-jawed father.

As though the father himself had snubbed her for some unimaginable familiarity the White Linen Nurse winced back in hopeless confusion. Just for sheer shock, short-circuited with fatigue, a big tear rolled slowly down one pink cheek.

Instantly to the edge of her seat the Little Girl jerked herself forward. "Don't cry, Pretty!" she whispered. "Don't cry! It's my legs. I've got fat iron braces on my legs. And people don't like to hold me!"

Half the professional smile came flashing back to the White Linen Nurse's mouth.

"Oh, I just adore holding people with iron braces on their legs," she affirmed, and, leaning over the back of the seat, proceeded with absolutely perfect mechanical tenderness to gather the poor, puny, surprised little body into her own strong, shapely arms. Then dutifully snuggling her shoulder to meet the stubborn little shoulder that refused to snuggle, to it, and dutifully easing her knees to suit the stubborn little knees that refused to be eased, she settled down resignedly in her seat again to await the return of the Senior Surgeon. "There! There! There!" she began quite instinctively to croon and pat.

"Don't say 'There! There!'" wailed the Little Girl peevishly. Her body was suddenly stiff as a ram-rod. "Don't say 'There! There!' If you've got to make any noise at all, say 'Here! Here!'"

"Here! Here!" droned the White Linen Nurse. "Here! Here! Here! Here!" On and on and interminably on, "Here! Here! Here! Here!"

At the end of about the three-hundred-and-forty-seventh "Here!" the Little Girl's body relaxed, and she reached up two fragile fingers to close the White Linen Nurse's mouth. "There! That will do," she sighed contentedly. "I feel better now. Father does tire me so."

"Father tires - *you*?" gasped the White Linen Nurse. The giggle that followed the gasp was not in the remotest degree professional. "Father tires *you*?" she repeated accusingly. "Why, you silly Little Girl! Can't you see it's you that makes Father so everlastingly tired?" Impulsively with her one free hand she turned the Little Girl's listless face to the light. "What makes you call your nice father 'Fat Father'?" she asked with real curiosity. "What makes you? He isn't fat at all. He's just big. Why, what ever possesses you to call him 'Fat Father,' I say? Can't you see how mad it makes him?"

"Why, of course it made him mad!" said the Little Girl with plainly reviving interest. Thrilled with astonishment at the White Linen Nurse's apparent stupidity she straightened up perkily with inordinately sparkling eyes. "Why, of course it makes him mad!" she explained briskly. "That's why I do it! Why, my Parpa - never even looks at me - unless I make him mad!"

"S - sh!" said the White Linen Nurse. "Why, you mustn't ever say a thing like that! Why, your Marma wouldn't like you to say a thing like that!"

Jerking bumpily back against the White Linen Nurse's unprepared shoulder the Little Girl prodded a pallid finger-tip into the White Linen Nurse's vivid cheek. "Silly - Pink and White - Nursie!" she chuckled, "Don't you know there *isn't* any Marma?" Cackling with delight over her own superior knowledge she folded her little arms and began to rock herself convulsively to and fro.

"Why, stop!" cried the White Linen Nurse. "Now you stop! Why, you wicked little creature laughing like that about your poor dead mother! Why, just think how bad it would make your poor Parpa feel!"

With instant sobriety the Little Girl stopped rocking, and stared perplexedly into the White Linen Nurse's shocked eyes. Her own little face was all wrinkled up with earnestness.

"But the Parpa - didn't like the Marma!" she explained painstakingly. "The Parpa - *never* liked the Marma! That's why he doesn't like me! I heard Cook telling the Ice Man once when I wasn't more than ten minutes old!"

Desperately with one straining hand the White Linen Nurse

stretched her fingers across the Little Girl's babbling mouth. Equally desperately, with the other hand, she sought to divert the Little Girl's mind by pushing the fur cap back from her frizzly red hair, and loosening her sumptuous coat, and jerking down vainly across two painfully obtrusive white ruffles, the awkwardly short, hideously bright little purple dress.

"I think your cap is too hot," she began casually, and then proceeded with increasing vivacity and conviction to the objects that worried her most. "And those - those ruffles," she protested, "they don't look a bit nice being so long!" Resentfully she rubbed an edge of the purple dress between her fingers. "And a little girl like you, - with such bright red hair, - oughtn't to wear - purple!" she admonished with real concern.

"Now whites and blues - and little soft pussy-cat grays -"

Mumblingly through her finger-muzzled mouth the Little Girl burst into explanations again.

"Oh, but when I wear gray," she persisted, "the Parpa - never sees me! But when I wear purple he cares, - he cares - most awfully!" she boasted with a bitter sort of triumph. "Why when I wear purple and frizz my hair hard enough, - no matter who's there, or anything, - he'll stop right off short in the middle of whatever he's doing - and rear right up so perfectly beautiful and mad and glorious - and holler right out 'For Heaven's sake, take that colored Sunday supplement away!'"

"Your Father's nervous," suggested the White Linen Nurse.

Almost tenderly the Little Girl reached up and drew the White Linen Nurse's ear close down to her own snuggling lips.

"Damned nervous!" she confided laconically.

Quite against all intention the White Linen Nurse giggled. Floundering to recover her dignity she plunged into a new error. "Poor little dev - ," she began.

"Yes," sighed the Little Girl complacently. "That's just what the Parpa calls me." Fervidly she clasped her little hands together. "Yes, if I can only make him mad enough daytimes," she asserted, "then at night when he thinks I'm all asleep he comes and stands by my cribby-house like a great black shadow-bear and shakes and shakes his most beautiful head and says, 'Poor little devil - poor little devil.' Oh, if I can only make him mad enough daytimes!" she cried out ecstatically.

"Why, you naughty little thing!" scolded the White Linen Nurse with an unmistakable catch in her voice. "Why, you - naughty - naughty - little thing!"

Like the brush of a butterfly's wing the child's hand grazed the White Linen Nurse's cheek. "I'm a lonely little thing," she confided wistfully. "Oh, I'm an awfully lonely little thing!" With really shocking abruptness the old malicious smile came twittering back to her mouth. "But I'll get even with the Parpa yet!" she threatened joyously, reaching out with pliant fingers to count the buttons on the White Linen Nurse's dress. "Oh, I'll get even with the Parpa yet!" In the midst of the passionate assertion her rigid little mouth relaxed in a most mild and innocent yawn.

"Oh, of course," she yawned, "on wash days and ironing days and every other work day in the week he has to be away cutting up people 'cause that's his lawful business. But Sundays, when he doesn't really need to at all, he goes off to some kind of a green, grassy club - all day long - and plays golf."

Very palpably her eyelids began to droop. "Where was I?" she asked sharply. "Oh, yes, 'the green, grassy club.' Well, when I die," she faltered, "I'm going to die specially on some Sunday when there's a big golf game, - so he'll just naturally have to give it up and stay home and - amuse me - and help arrange the flowers. The Parpa's crazy about flowers. So am I," she added broodingly. "I raised almost a geranium once. But the Parpa threw it out. It was a good geranium, too. All it did was just to drip the tiniest-teeniest bit over a book and a writing and somebody's brains in a dish. He threw it at a cat. It was a good cat, too. All it did was to -"

A little jerkily her drooping head bobbed forward and then back again. Her heavy eyes were almost tight shut by this time, and after a moment's silence her lips began moving dumbly like one at silent devotions. "I'm making a little poem, now," she confided at last. "It's about - you and me. It's a sort of a little prayer." Very, very softly she began to repeat.

> Now I sit me down to nap
> All curled up in a Nursie's lap,
> If *she* should die before I wake -

Abruptly she stopped and stared up suspiciously into the White Linen Nurse's eyes. "Ha!" she mocked, "you thought I was going to say 'If I should die before I wake,' - didn't you? *Well, I'm not*!"

"It would have been more generous," acknowledged the White Linen Nurse.

Very stiffly the Little Girl pursed her lips. "It's plenty generous enough - when it's all done!" she said severely. "And I'll thank you, - Miss Malgregor, - not to interrupt me again!" With excessive deliberateness she went back to the first line of her poem and began all over again,

Now I sit me down to nap,
All curled up in a Nursie's lap,
If *she* should die before I wake,
Give her - give her ten cents - for Jesus' sake!

"Why that's a - a cunning little prayer," yawned the White Linen Nurse. Most certainly of course she would have smiled if the yawn hadn't caught her first. But now in the middle of the yawn it was a great deal easier to repeat the "very cunning" than to force her lips into any new expression. "Very cunning -

very cunning," she kept crooning conscientiously.

Modestly like some other successful authors the Little Girl flapped her eyelids languidly open and shut for three or four times before she acknowledged the compliment. "Oh, cunning as any of 'em," she admitted off-handishly. Only once again did she open either mouth or eyes, and this time it was merely one eye and half a mouth. "Do my fat iron braces - hurt you?" she mumbled drowsily.

"Yes, a little," conceded the White Linen Nurse.

"Ha! They hurt me - all the time!" gibed the Little Girl.

Five minutes later, the child who didn't particularly care about being held, and the girl who didn't particularly care about holding her, were fast asleep in each other's arms, - a naughty, nagging, restive little hornet all hushed up and a-dream in the heart of a pink wild-rose!

Stalking out of the house in his own due time the Senior Surgeon reared back aghast at the sight.

"Well - I'll be hanged!" he muttered. "Most everlastingly hanged! Wonder what they think this is? A somnolent kindergarten show? Talk about fiddling while Rome burns!"

Awkwardly, on the top step, he struggled alone into his cumbersome coat. Every tingling nerve in his body, every shuddering sensibility, was racked to its utmost capacity over the distressing scenes he had left behind him in the big house. Back in that luxuriant sickroom, Youth Incarnate lay stripped, root, branch, leaf, bud, blossom, fruit, of All its manhood's promise. Back in that erudite library, Culture Personified, robbed of all its fine philosophy, sat babbling illiterate street-curses into its quivering hands. Back in that exquisite pink and gold boudoir, Blonded Fashion, ravished for once of all its artistry, ran stumbling round and round in interminable circles like a disheveled hag. In shrill crescendos and discordant basses, with heartpiercing jaggedness, with blood-curdling raspishness, each one, boy, father, mother, meddlesome relative, competent or incompetent assistant, indiscriminate servant, filing his separate sorrow into the Senior Surgeon's tortured ears!

With one of those sudden revulsions to materialism which is liable to overwhelm any man who delves too long at a time in the brutally unconventional issues of life and death, the Senior Surgeon stepped down into the subtle, hyacinth-scented sunshine with every latent human greed in his body clamoring for expression - before it, too, should be hurtled into oblivion. "Eat, you fool, and drink, you fool, and be merry, - you fool, - for to-morrow - *even you, - Lendicott R. Faber - may have to die*!" brawled and re-brawled through his mind like a ribald phonograph tune.

At the edge of the bottom step a precipitous lilac branch that must have budded and bloomed in a single hour smote him stingingly across his cheek. "Laggard!" taunted the lilac branch.

With the first crunching grit of gravel under his feet, something transcendently naked and unashamed that was neither Brazen Sorrow nor Brazen Pain thrilled across his startled consciousness. Over the rolling, marshy meadow, beyond the succulent willow-hedge that hid the winding river, up from some fluent, slim canoe, out from a chorus of virile young tenor voices, a little passionate Love Song - divinely tender - most incomparably innocent - came stealing palpitantly forth into that inflammable Spring world without a single vestige of accompaniment on it!

> Kiss me, Sweet, the Spring is here,
> And Love is Lord of you and me,
> There's no bird in brake or brere,
> But to his little mate sings he,
> "Kiss me, Sweet, the Spring is here
> And Love is Lord of you - and me!"

Wrenched like a sob out of his own lost youth the Senior Surgeon's faltering college memories took up the old refrain.

As I go singing, to my dear,
"Kiss me, Sweet, the Spring is here,
And Love is Lord of you and me!"

Just for an instant a dozen long-forgotten pictures lanced themselves poignantly into his brain, - dingy, uncontrovertible old recitation rooms where young ideas flashed bright and futile as parade swords, - elm-shaded slopes where lithe young bodies lolled on green velvet grasses to expound their harshest cynicisms! Book-history, book-science, book-economics, book-love, - all the paper passion of all the paper poets swaggering imperiously on boyish lips that would have died a thousand bashful deaths before the threatening imminence of a real girl's kiss! Magic days, with Youth the one glittering, positive treasure on the Tree of Life - and Woman still a mystery!

"Woman a mystery?" Harshly the phrase ripped through the Senior Surgeon's brain. Croakingly in that instant all the grim gray scientific years re-overtook him, swamped him, strangled him. "Woman a *mystery*? Oh ye Gods! And Youth? Bah! Youth, - a mere tinsel tinkle on a rotting Christmas tree!"

Furiously with renewed venom he turned and threw his weight again upon the stubbornly resistant crank of his automobile.

Vaguely disturbed by the noise and vibration the White Linen Nurse opened her big, drowsy, blue eyes upon him.

"Don't - jerk - it - so!" she admonished hazily, "You'll wake the Little Girl!"

"Well, what about my convenience, I'd like to know?" snapped the Senior Surgeon in some astonishment.

Heavily the White Linen Nurse's lashes shadowed down again across her sleep-flushed cheeks.

"Oh, never mind - about - that," she mumbled non-concernedly.

"Oh, for Heaven's sake - wake up there!" bellowed the Senior Surgeon above the sudden roar of his engine.

Adroitly for a man of his bulk he ran around the radiator and jumped into his seat. Joggled unmercifully into wakefulness, the Little Girl greeted his return with a generous if distinctly non-tactful demonstration of affection. Grabbing the unwitting fingers of his momentarily free hand she tapped them proudly against the White Linen Nurse's plump pink cheek.

"See! I call her 'Peach'!" she boasted joyously with all the triumphant air of one who felt assured that mental discrimination such as this could not possibly fail to impress even a person so naturally obtuse as - a father.

"Don't be foolish!" snarled the Senior Surgeon.

"Who? Me?" gasped the White Linen Nurse in a perfect agony of confusion.

"Yes! You!" snapped the Senior Surgeon explosively half an hour later after interminable miles of absolute silence - and dingy yellow field-stubble - and bare brown alder bushes.

Truly out of the ascetic habit of his daily life, "where no rain was," as the Bible would put it, it did seem to him distinctly foolish, not to say careless, not to say out and out incendiary, for any girl to go blushing her way like a fire-brand through a world so palpably populated by young men whose heads were tow, and hearts indisputably tinder, rather than tender.

"Yes! You!" he reasserted vehemently at the end of another silent mile.

Then plainly begrudging this second inexcusable interruption of his most vital musings concerning Spinal Meningitis he scowled his way savagely back again into his own grimly established trend of thought.

Excited by so much perfectly good silence that nobody seemed to be using the Little Crippled Girl ventured gallantly forth once more into the hazardous conversational land of grown-ups.

"Father?" she experimented cautiously with most commendable discretion.

Fathoms deep in abstraction the Senior Surgeon stared unheeding into the whizzing black road. Pulses and temperatures and blood-pressures were seething in his mind; and sharp sticks and jagged stones and the general possibilities of a puncture; and murmurs of the heart and râles of the lungs; and a most unaccountable knock-knock-knocking in the engine; and the probable relation of middle-ear disease; and the perfectly positive symptoms of optic neuritis; and a damned funny squeak in the steering gear!

"Father?" the Little Girl persisted valiantly.

To add to his original concentration the Senior Surgeon's linen collar began to chafe him maddeningly under his chin. The annoyance added two scowls to his already blackly furrowed face, and at least ten miles an hour to his running time; but nothing whatsoever to his conversational ability.

"Father!" the Little Girl whimpered with faltering courage. Then panic-stricken, as wiser people have been before her, over the dreadful spookish remoteness of a perfectly normal human being who refuses either to answer or even to notice your wildest efforts at communication, she raised her waspish voice in its shrillest, harshest war-cry. "Fat Father! *Fat Father! F-a-t F-a-t-h-e-r!*" she screeched out frenziedly at the top of her lungs.

The gun-shot agony of a wounded rabbit was in the cry, the last gurgling gasp of strangulation under a murderer's reeking fingers, - catastrophe unspeakable, - disaster now irrevocable!

Clamping down his brakes with a wrench that almost tore the insides out of his engine the Senior Surgeon brought the great car to a staggering standstill.

"What is it?" he cried in real terror. "What is it?"

Limply the Little Girl stretched down from the White Linen Nurse's lap till she could nick her toe against the shiniest woodwork in sight. Altogether aimlessly her small chin began to burrow deeper and deeper into her big fur collar.

"For Heaven's sake, what do you want?" demanded the Senior Surgeon. Even yet along his spine the little nerves crinkled with shock and apprehension. "For Heaven's sake what do you want?"

Helplessly the child lifted her turbid eyes to his. With unmistakable appeal her tiny hand went clutching out at one of the big buttons on his coat. Desperately for an instant she rummaged through her brain for some remotely adequate answer to this most thunderous question, - and then retreated precipitously as usual to the sacristy of her own imagination.

"All the birds *were* there, Father!" she confided guilelessly. "All the birds *were* there, - with yellow feathers instead of hair! And bumblebees - crocheted in the trees. And -"

Short of complete annihilation there was no satisfying vengeance whatsoever that the Senior Surgeon's exploding passion could wreak upon his offspring. Complete annihilation being unfeasible at the moment he merely climbed laboriously out of the car, re-cranked the engine, climbed laboriously back into his place and started on his way once more. All the red blustering rage was stripped completely from him. Startlingly rigid, startlingly white, his face was like the death-mask of a pirate.

Pleasantly excited by she-didn't-know-exactly-what, the Little Girl resumed her beloved falsetto chant, rhythmically all the while with her puny iron-braced legs beating the tune into the White Linen Nurse's tender flesh.

All the birds were there
With yellow feathers instead of hair,
And bumblebees crocheted in the trees
And - and - all the birds were there,
With yellow feathers instead of hair,
And -

Frenziedly as a runaway horse trying to escape from its own pursuing harness and carriage the Senior Surgeon poured increasing speed into both his own pace and the pace of his tormentor. Up hill, - down dale, - screeching through rocky echoes, - swishing through blue-green spruce-lands, - dodging indomitable boulders, - grazing lax, treacherous embankments, - the great car scuttled homeward. Huddled behind his steering wheel like a warrior behind his shield, every body-muscle taut with strain, every facial muscle diabolically calm, the Senior Surgeon met and parried successively each fresh onslaught of yard, rod, mile.

Then suddenly in the first precipitous descent of a mighty hill the whole earth seemed to drop out from under the car. Down-down-down with incredible swiftness and smoothness the great machine went diving towards abysmal space! Up-up-up with incredible bumps and bouncings, trees, bushes, stonewalls went rushing to the sky!

Gasping surprisedly towards the Senior Surgeon the White Linen Nurse saw his grim mouth yank round abruptly in her direction as it yanked sometimes in the operating-room with some sharp, incisive order of life or death. Instinctively she leaned forward for the message.

Not over-loud but strangely distinct the words slapped back into her straining ears.

"If - it will rest your face any - to look scared - by all means - do so! I've lost control of the machine!" called the Senior Surgeon sardonically across the roar of the wind.

The phrase excited the White Linen Nurse but it did not remotely frighten her. She was not in the habit of seeing the Senior Surgeon lose control of any situation. Merely intoxicated with speed, delirious with ozone, she snatched up the Little Girl close, to her breast.

"We're flying!" she cried. "We're dropping from a parachute! We're - !"

Swoopingly like a sled striking glare, level ice the great car swerved from the bottom of the hill into a soft rolling meadow. Instantly from every conceivable direction, like foes in ambush, trees, stumps, rocks reared up in threatening defiance.

Tighter and tighter the White Linen Nurse crushed the Little Girl to her breast. Louder and louder she called in the Little Girl's ear.

"Scream!" she shouted. *"There might be a bump! Scream louder than a bump! Scream! Scream! Scream!"*

In that first over-whelming, nerve-numbing, heart-crunching terror of his whole life as the great car tilted up against a stone, - plowed down into the mushy edge of a marsh, - and skidded completely round, *crash-bang* - into a tree, it was the last sound that the Senior Surgeon heard, - the sound of a woman and child screeching th eir lungsout in diabolical exultancy!

CHAPTER V

When the White Linen Nurse found anything again she found herself lying perfectly flat on her back in a reasonably comfortable nest of grass and leaves. Staring inquisitively up into the sky she thought she noticed a slight black and blue discoloration towards the west, but more than that, much to her relief, the firmament did not seem to be seriously injured. The earth, she feared had not escaped so easily. Even way off somewhere near the tip of her fingers the ground was as sore – as sore - as could be - under her touch. Impulsively to her dizzy eyes the hot tears started, to think that now, tired as she was, she should have to jump right up in another minute or two and attend to the poor earth. Fortunately for any really strenuous emergency that might arise there seemed to be nothing about her own body that hurt at all except a queer, persistent little pain in her cheek. Not until the Little Crippled Girl's dirt-smouched face intervened between her own staring eyes and the sky did she realize that the pain in her cheek was a pinch.

"Wake up! Wake up!" scolded the Little Crippled Girl shrilly. "Naughty - Pink and White Nursie! I wanted to hear the bump! You screamed so loud I couldn't hear the bump!"

With excessive caution the White Linen Nurse struggled up at last to a sitting posture, and gazed perplexedly around her.

It seemed to be a perfectly pleasant field, - acres and acres of mild old grass tottering palsiedly down to watch some skittish young violets and bluets frolic in and out of a giggling brook. Up the field? Up the field? Hazily the White Linen Nurse ground her knuckles into her incredulous eyes. Up the field, just beyond them, the great empty automobile stood amiably at rest. From the general appearance of the stone-wall at the top of the little grassy slope it was palpably evident that the car had attempted certain vain acrobatic feats before its failing momentum had forced it into the humiliating ranks of the back-sliders.

Still grinding her knuckles into her eyes the White Linen Nurse turned back to the Little Girl. Under the torn, twisted sable cap one little eye was hidden completely, but the other eye loomed up rakish and bruised as a prizefighter's. One sable sleeve was wrenched disastrously from its arm-hole, and along the edge of the vivid little purple skirt the ill-favored white ruffles seemed to have raveled out into hopeless yards and yards and yards of Hamburg embroidery.

A trifle self-consciously the Little Girl began to gather herself together.

"We - we seem to have fallen out of something!" she confided with the air of one who halves a most precious secret.

"Yes, I know," said the White Linen Nurse. "But what has become of - your Father?"

Worriedly for an instant the Little Girl sat scanning the remotest corners of the field. Then abruptly with a gasp of real relief she began to explore with cautious fingers the geographical outline of her black eye.

"Oh, never mind about Father," she asserted cheerfully. "I guess - I guess he got mad and went home."

"Yes - I know," mused the White Linen Nurse. "But it doesn't seem - probable."

"Probable?" mocked the Little Girl most disagreeably. Then suddenly her little hand went shooting out towards the stranded automobile.

"Why, there he is!" she screamed. "Under the car! Oh, Look - Look - Lookey!"

Laboriously the White Linen Nurse scrambled to her knees. Desperately she tried to ram her fingers like a clog into the whirling dizziness round her temples.

"Oh, my God! Oh, my God! What's the dose for anybody under a car?" she babbled idiotically.

Then with a really herculean effort, - both mental and physical, she staggered to her feet, and started for the automobile.

But her knees gave out, and wilting down to the grass she tried to crawl along on all-fours, till straining wrists sent her back to her feet again.

Whenever she tried to walk the Little Girl walked, - whenever she tried to crawl the Little Girl crawled.

"Isn't it fun!" the shrill childish voice piped persistently. "Isn't it just like playing ship-wreck!"

When they reached the car both woman and child were too utterly exhausted with breathlessness to do anything except just sit down on the ground and - stare.

Sure enough under that monstrous, immovable looking machine the Senior Surgeon's body lay rammed face-down deep, deep into the grass.

It was the Little Girl who recovered her breath first.

"I think he's dead!" she volunteered sagely. "His legs look –

awfully dead - to me!" Only excitement was in the statement. It took a second or two for her little mind to make any particularly personal application of such excitement. "I hadn't - exactly - planned - on having him dead!" she began with imperious resentment. A threat of complete emotional collapse zig-zagged suddenly across her face. "I won't have him dead! I won't! I *won't*!" she screamed out stormily.

In the amazing silence that ensued the White Linen Nurse gathered her trembling knees up into the circle of her arms and sat there staring at the Senior Surgeon's prostrate body, and rocking herself feebly to and fro in a futile effort to collect her scattered senses.

"Oh, if some one would only tell me what to do, - I know I could do it! Oh, I know I could do it! If some one would only tell me what to do!" she kept repeating helplessly.

Cautiously the Little Girl crept forward on her hands and knees to the edge of the car and peered speculatively through the great yellow wheel-spokes. "Father!" she faltered in almost inaudible gentleness. "Father!" she pleaded in perfectly impotent whisper.

Impetuously the White Linen Nurse scrambled to her own hands and knees and jostled the Little Girl aside.

"Fat Father!" screamed the White Linen Nurse. "Fat Father! Fat Father! *Fat Father!"* she gibed and taunted with the one call she knew that had never yet failed to rouse him.

Perceptibly across the Senior Surgeon's horridly quiet shoulders a little twitch wrinkled and was gone again.

"Oh, his heart!" gasped the White Linen Nurse. "I must find his heart!"

Throwing herself prone upon the cool meadowy ground and frantically reaching out under the running board of the car to her full arm's length she began to rummage awkwardly hither and yon beneath the heavy weight of the man in the desperate hope of feeling a heart-beat.

"Ouch! You tickle me!" spluttered the Senior Surgeon weakly.

Rolling back quickly with fright and relief the White Linen Nurse burst forth into one maddening cackle of hysterical laughter. "Ha! Ha! Ha!" she giggled. "Hi! Hi! Titter! Titter! Titter!"

Perplexedly at first but with increasing abandon the Little Girl's voice took up the same idiotic refrain. "Ha-Ha-Ha," she choked. And "Hi-Hi-Hi!" And "Titter! Titter! Titter!"

With an agonizing jerk of his neck the Senior Surgeon rooted his mud-gagged mouth a half inch further towards free and spontaneous speech. Very laboriously, very painstakingly, he spat out one by one two stones and a wisp of ground pine and a brackish, prickly tickle of stale golden-rod.

"Blankety-blank-blank - BLANK!" he announced in due time, "Blankety-blank-blank-blank - BLANK! Maybe when you two - blankety-blank - imbeciles have got through your blankety-blank cackling you'll have the - blankety-blank decency to save my - my blankety-blank-blank - blank - *blank-blank* life!"

"Ha! Ha! Ha!" persisted the poor helpless White Linen Nurse with the tears streaming down her cheeks.

"Hi! Hi! Hi!" snickered the poor Little Girl through her hiccoughs.

Feeling hopelessly crushed under two tons and a half of car, the Senior Surgeon closed his eyes for death. No man of his weight, he felt quite sure, could reasonably expect to survive many minutes longer the apoplectic, blood-red rage that pounded in his ear-drums. Through his tight-closed eyelids very, very slowly a red glow seemed to permeate. He thought it was the fires of Hell. Opening his eyes to meet his fate like a man he found himself staring impudently close instead into the White Linen Nurse's furiously flushed face that lay cuddled on one plump cheek staring impudently close at him.

"Why - why - get out!" gasped the Senior Surgeon.

Very modestly the White Linen Nurse's face retreated a little further into its blushes.

"Yes, I know," she protested. "But I'm all through giggling now. I'm sorry - I'm -"

In sheer apprehensiveness the Senior Surgeon's features crinkled wincingly from brow to chin as though struggling vainly to retreat from the appalling proximity of the girl's face.

"Your - eyelashes - are too long," he complained querulously.

"Eh?" jerked the White Linen Nurse's face. "Is it your brain that's hurt? Oh, sir, do you think it's your brain that's hurt?"

"It's my stomach!" snapped the Senior Surgeon. "I tell you I 'm not hurt, - I'm just - squashed! I'm paralyzed! If I can't get this car off me -"

"Yes, that's just it," beamed the White Linen Nurse's face. "That's just what I crawled in here to find out, - how to get the car off you. That's just what I want to find out. I could run for help, of course, - only I couldn't run, 'cause my knees are so wobbly. It would take hours - and the car might start or burn up or something while I was gone. But you don't seem to be caught anywhere on the machinery," she added more brightly, "it only seems to be sitting on you. So if I could only get the car off you! But it's so heavy. I had no idea it would be so heavy. Could I take it apart, do you think? Is there any one place where I could begin at the beginning and take it all apart?"

"Take it apart - Hell!" groaned the Senior Surgeon.

A little twitch of defiance flickered across the White Linen Nurse's face. "All the same," she asserted stubbornly, "if some one would only tell me what to do - I know I could do it!"

Horridly from some unlocatable quarter of the engine an alarming littletremor quickened suddenly and was hushed again.

"Get out of here - quick!" stormed the Senior Surgeon's ghastly face.

"I won't!" said the White Linen Nurse's face. "Until you tell me - what to do!"

Brutally for an instant the ingenuous blue eyes and the cynical gray eyes battled each other.

"*Can* you do what you're told?" faltered the Senior Surgeon.

"Oh, yes," said the White Linen Nurse.

"I mean can you do exactly - what you're told?" gasped the Senior Surgeon. "Can you follow directions, I mean? Can you follow them - explicitly? Or are you one of those people who listens only to her own judgment?"

"Oh, but I haven't got any - judgment," protested the White Linen Nurse.

Palpably in the Senior Surgeon's blood-shot eyes the leisurely seeming diagnosis leaped to precipitous conclusions.

"Then get out of here - quick - for God's sake - and get to work!" he ordered.

Cautiously the White Linen Nurse jerked herself back into freedom and crawled around and stared at the Senior Surgeon through the wheel-spokes again. Like one worrying out some intricate mathematical problem his mental strain was pulsing visibly through his closed eyelids.

"Yes, sir?" prodded the White Linen Nurse.

"Keep still!" snapped the Senior Surgeon. "I've got to think," he said. "I've got to work it out! All in a moment you've got to learn to run the car. All in a moment! It's awful!"

"Oh, I don't mind, sir," affirmed the White Linen Nurse serenely.

Frenziedly the Senior Surgeon rooted one cheek into the mud again. "You don't - *mind*?" he groaned. "You don't - *mind*? Why, you've got to learn - everything! Everything - from - the very beginning!"

"Oh, that's all right, sir," crooned the White Linen Nurse.

Ominously from somewhere a horrid sound creaked again. The Senior Surgeon did not stop to argue any further.

"Now come here," ordered the Senior Surgeon. "I'm going to - I'm going to -" Startlingly his voice weakened, - trailed off into nothingness, - and rallied suddenly with exaggerated bruskness. "Look here now! For Heaven's sake use your brains! I'm going to dictate to you - very slowly - one thing at a time - just what to do!"

Quite astonishingly the White Linen Nurse sank down on her knees and began to grin at him. "Oh, no, sir," she said. "I couldn't do it that way, - not 'one thing at a time.' Oh, no indeed, sir! No!" Absolute finality was in her voice, - the inviolable stubbornness of the perfectly good-natured person.

"You'll do it the way I tell you to!" roared the Senior Surgeon struggling vainly to ease one shoulder or stretch one knee-joint.

"Oh, no, sir," beamed the White Linen Nurse. "Not one thing at a time! Oh, no, I couldn't do it that way! Oh, no, sir, I won't do it that way - one thing at a time," she persisted hurriedly. "Why, you might faint away or something might happen - right in the middle of it - right between one direction and another - and I wouldn't know at all - what to turn on or off next - and it might take off one of your legs, you know, or an arm. Oh, no, - not one thing at a time!"

"Good-by - then," croaked the Senior Surgeon. "I'm as good as dead now." A single shudder went through him, - a last futile effort to stretch himself.

"Good-by," said the White Linen Nurse. "Good-by, sir. - I'd heaps rather have you die - perfectly whole - like that - of your own accord - than have me run the risk of starting the car full-tilt and chopping you up so - or dragging you off so - that you didn't find it convenient to tell me - how to stop the car."

"You're a - a - a -" spluttered the Senior Surgeon indistinguishably.

"Crinkle-crackle," went that mysterious, horrid sound from somewhere in the machinery.

"Oh my God!" surrendered the Senior Surgeon. "Do it your own - damned way! Only - only -" His voice cracked raspingly.

"Steady! Steady there!" said the White Linen Nurse. Except for a sudden odd pucker at the end of her nose her expression was still perfectly serene. "Now begin at the beginning," she begged. "Quick! Tell me everything - just the way I must do it! Quick - quick - quick!"

Twice the Senior Surgeon's lips opened and shut with a vain effort to comply with her request.

"But you can't do it," he began all over again. "It isn't possible. You haven't got the mind!"

"Maybe I haven't," said the White Linen Nurse. "But I've got the memory. Hurry!"

"Creak," said the funny little something in the machinery. "Creak - drip - bubble!"

"Oh, get in there quick!" surrendered the Senior Surgeon. "Sit down behind the wheel!" he shouted after her flying footsteps. "Are you there? For God's sake - are you there? Do you see those two little levers where your right hand comes? For God's sake - don't you know what a lever is? Quick now! Do just what I tell you!"

A little jerkily then, but very clearly, very concisely, the Senior Surgeon called out to the White Linen Nurse just how every lever, every pedal should be manipulated to start the car!

Absolutely accurately, absolutely indelibly the White Linen Nurse visualized each separate detail in her abnormally retentive mind!

"But you can't - possibly remember it!" groaned the Senior Surgeon. "You can't - possibly! And probably the damn car's *bust* and won't start - anyway - and - !" Abruptly the speech ended in a guttural snarl of despair.

"Don't be a - blight!" screamed the White Linen Nurse. "I've never forgotten anything yet, sir!"

Very tensely she straightened up suddenly in her seat. Her expression was no longer even remotely pleasant. Along her sensitive, fluctuant nostrils the casual crinkle of distaste and suspicion had deepened suddenly into sheer dilating terror.

"Left foot - press down - hard - left pedal!" she began to sing-song to herself.

"No! *Right* foot! - *right* foot!" corrected the Little Girl blunderingly from somewhere close in the grass.

"Inside lever - pull - way - back!" persisted the White Linen Nurse resolutely as she switched on the current.

"No! *Outside* lever! *Outside! Outside*!" contradicted the Little Girl.

"Shut your darned mouth!" screeched the White Linen Nurse, her hand on the throttle as she tried the self starter.

Bruised as he was, wretched, desperately endangered there under the car the Senior Surgeon could almost have grinned at the girl's terse, unconscious mimicry of his own most venomous tones.

Then with all the forty-eight lusty, ebullient years of his life snatched from his lips like an untasted cup, and one single noxious, death-flavored second urged, - forced, - crammed down his choking throat, he felt the great car quicken and start.

"God!" said the Senior Surgeon. Just "God!" The God of mud, he meant! The God of brackish grass! The God of a man lying still hopeful under more than two tons' weight of unaccountable mechanism, with a novice in full command.

Up in her crimson leather cushions, free-lunged, free-limbed, the White Linen Nurse heard the smothered cry. Clear above the whirr of wheels, the whizz of clogs, the one word sizzled like a red-hot poker across her chattering consciousness. Tingling through the grasp of her fingers on the vibrating wheel, stinging through the sole of her foot that hovered over the throbbing clutch, she sensed the agonized appeal. "Short lever - spark - long lever - gas!" she persisted resolutely. "It must be right! It must!"

Jerkily then, and blatantly unskilfully, with riotous puffs and spinning of wheels, the great car started, - faltered, - balked a bit, - then dragged crushingly across the Senior Surgeon's flattened body, and with a great wanton burst of speed tore down the sloping meadow into the brook - rods away. Clamping down the brakes with a wrench and a racket like the smash of a machine-shop the White Linen Nurse jumped out into the brook, and with one wild terrified glance behind her staggered back up the long grassy slope to the Senior Surgeon.

Mechanically through her wooden-feeling lips she forced the greeting that sounded most cheerful to her. "It's not much fun, sir, - running an auto," she gasped. "I don't believe I'd like it!"

Half propped up on one elbow, - still dizzy with mental chaos, still paralyzed with physical inertia, - the Senior Surgeon lay staring blankly all around him. Indifferently for an instant his stare included the White Linen Nurse. Then glowering suddenly at something way beyond her, his face went perfectly livid.

"Good God! The - the car's on fire!" he mumbled.

"Yes, sir," said the White Linen Nurse. "Why! Didn't you know it, sir?"

CHAPTER VI

Headlong the Senior Surgeon pitched over on the grass, - his last vestige of self-control stripped from him, - horror unspeakable racking him sobbingly from head to toe.

Whimperingly the Little Girl came crawling to him, and settling down close at his feet began with her tiny lace handkerchief to make futile dabs at the mud-stains on his gray silk stockings. "Never mind, Father," she coaxed, "we'll get you clean sometime."

Nervously the White Linen Nurse bethought her of the brook. "Oh, wait a minute, sir - and I'll get you a drink of water!" she pleaded.

Bruskly the Senior Surgeon's hand jerked out and grabbed at her skirt.

"Don't leave me!" he begged. "For God's sake - don't leave me!"

Weakly he struggled up again and sat staring piteously at the blazing car. His unrelinquished clutch on the White Linen Nurse's skirt brought her sinking softly down beside him like a collapsed balloon. Together they sat and watched the gaseous yellow flames shoot up into the sky.

"It's pretty, isn't it?" piped the Little Girl.

"Eh?" groaned the Senior Surgeon.

"Father," persisted the shrill little voice. "Father, - do people ever burn up?"

"*Eh?*" gasped the Senior Surgeon. Brutally the harsh, shuddering sobs began to rack and tear again through his great chest.

"There! There!" crooned the White Linen Nurse, struggling desperately to her knees. "Let me get - everybody - a drink of water."

Again the Senior Surgeon's unrelinquished clutch on her skirt jerked her back to the place beside him.

"I said *not to leave me*!" he snapped out as roughly as he jerked.

Before the affrighted look in the White Linen Nurse's face a sheepish, mirthless grin flickered across one corner of his mouth.

"Lord! But I'm shaken!" he apologized. "Me - of all people!" Painfully the red blood mounted to his cheeks. "Me - of all people!" Bluntly he forced the White Linen Nurse's reluctant gaze to meet his own. "Only yesterday," he persisted, "I did a laparotomy on a man who had only one chance in a hundred of pulling through - and I - I scolded him for fighting off his ether cone, - scolded him - I tell you!"

"Yes, I know," soothed the White Linen Nurse. "But -"

"But *nothing*!" growled the Senior Surgeon. "The fear of death? Bah! All my life I've scoffed at it! *Die*? Yes, of course, - when you have to, - but with no kick coming! Why, I've been wrecked in a typhoon in the Gulf of Mexico. And I didn't care! And I've lain for nine days more dead than alive in an Asiatic cholera camp. And I didn't care! And I've been locked into my office three hours with a raving maniac and a dynamite bomb. And I didn't care! And twice in a Pennsylvania mine disaster I've been the first man down the shaft. And I didn't care! And I've been shot, I tell you, - and I've been horse-trampled, - and I've been wolf-bitten. And I've never cared! But to-day - to-day -" Piteously all the pride and vigor wilted from his great shoulders, leaving him all huddled up like a woman, with his head on his knees. "But to-day, I've *got mine!*" he acknowledged brokenly.

Once again the White Linen Nurse tried to rise. "Oh, please, sir, let me get you a - drink of water," she suggested helplessly.

"I said *not to leave me!*" jerked the Senior Surgeon.

Perplexedly with big staring eyes the Little Crippled Girl glanced up at this strange fatherish person who sounded so suddenly small and scared like herself. Jealous instantly of her own prerogatives she dropped her futile labors on the mud-stained silk stockings and scrambled precipitously for the White Linen Nurse's lap where she nestled down finally after many gyrations, and sat glowering forth at all possible interlopers.

"Don't leave any of us!" she ordered with a peremptoriness not unmixed with supplication.

"Surely some one will see the fire and come and get us," conceded the Senior Surgeon.

"Yes - surely," mused the White Linen Nurse. Just at that moment she was mostly concerned with adjusting the curve of her shoulder to the curve of the Little Girl's head. "I could sit more comfortably," she suggested to the Senior Surgeon, "if you'd let go my skirt."

"Let go of your skirt? Who's touching your skirt?" gasped the Senior Surgeon incredulously. Once again the blood mounted darkly to his face. "I think I'll get up - and walk around a bit," he confided coldly.

"Do, sir," said the White Linen Nurse.

Ouchily with a tweak of pain through his sprained back the Senior Surgeon sat suddenly down again. "I sha'n't get up till I'm good and ready!" he attested.

"I wouldn't, sir," said the White Linen Nurse.

Very slowly, very complacently, all the while she kept right on renovating the Little Girl's personal appearance, smoothing a wrinkled stocking, tucking up obstreperous white ruffles, tugging down parsimonious purple hems, loosening a pinchy hook, tightening a wobbly button. Very slowly, very complacently the Little Girl drowsed off to sleep with her weazened little iron-cased legs stretched stiffly out before her. "Poor little legs! Poor little legs! Poor little legs!" crooned the White Linen Nurse.

"I don't know - as you need to - make a song about it!" winced the Senior Surgeon. "It's just about the crudest case of complete muscular atrophy that I've ever seen!"

Blandly the White Linen Nurse lifted her big blue eyes to his. "It wasn't her 'complete muscular atrophy' that I was thinking about!" she said. "It's her panties that are so unbecoming!"

"Eh?" jumped the Senior Surgeon.

"Poor little legs - poor little legs - poor little legs," resumed the White Linen Nurse droningly.

Very slowly, very complacently, all around them April kept right on - being April.

Very slowly, very complacently, all around them the grass kept On growing, and the trees kept right on budding. Very slowly, very complacently, all around them the blue sky kept right on fading into its early evening dove-colors.

Nothing brisk, nothing breathless, nothing even remotely hurried was there in all the landscape except just the brook, - and the flash of a bird, - and the blaze of the crackling automobile.

The White Linen Nurse's nostrils were smooth and calm with the lovely sappy scent of rabbit-nibbled maple bark and mud-wet arbutus buds. The White Linen Nurse's mind was full of sumptuous, succulent marsh marigolds, and fluffy white shad-bush blossoms.

The Senior Surgeon's nostrils were all puckered up with the stench of burning varnish. The Senior Surgeon's mind was full of the horrid thought that he'd forgotten to renew his automobile fire-insurance, - and that he had a sprained back, - and that his rival colleague had told him he didn't know how to run an auto anyway - and that the cook had given notice that morning, - and that he had a sprained back, - and that the moths had gnawed the knees out of his new dress suit, - and that the Superintendent of Nurses had had the audacity to send him a bunch of pink roses for his birthday, - and that the boiler in the kitchen leaked, - and that he had to go to Philadelphia the next day to read a paper on "Surgical Methods at the Battle of Waterloo," - and he hadn't even begun the paper yet, - and that he had a sprained back, - and that the wall-paper on his library hung in shreds and tatters waiting for him to decide between a French fresco effect and an early English paneling, - and that his little daughter was growing up in wanton ugliness under the care of coarse, indifferent hirelings, - and that the laundry robbed him weekly of at least five socks, - and that it would cost him fully seven thousand dollars to replace this car, - and that he had a sprained back!

"It's restful, isn't it?" cooed the White Linen Nurse.

"Isn't *what* restful?" glowered the Senior Surgeon.

"Sitting down!" said the White Linen Nurse.

Contemptuously the Senior Surgeon's mind ignored the interruption and reverted precipitously to its own immediate problem concerning the gloomy, black-walnut shadowed entrance hall of his great house, and how many yards of imported linoleum at $3.45 a yard it would take to recarpet the "damned hole," - and how it would have seemed anyway if - if he hadn't gone home - as usual to the horrid black-walnut shadows that night - but been carried home instead - feet first and - quite dead - dead, mind you, with a red necktie on, - and even the cook was out! And they wouldn't even know where to lay him - but might put him by mistake in that - in that - in his dead wife's dead - bed!

Altogether unconsciously a little fluttering sigh of ineffable contentment escaped the White Linen Nurse.

"I don't care how long we have to sit here and wait for help," she announced cheerfully, "because to-morrow, of course, I'll have to get up and begin all over again - and go to Nova Scotia."

"Go *where*?" lurched the Senior Surgeon.

"I'd thank you kindly, sir, not to jerk my skirt quite so hard!" said the White Linen Nurse just a trifle stiffly.

Incredulously once more the Senior Surgeon withdrew his detaining hand. "I'm not even touching your skirt!" he denied desperately. Nothing but denial and reiterated denial seemed to ease his self-esteem for an instant. "Why, for Heaven's sake, should I want to hold on to your skirt?" he demanded peremptorily. "What the deuce -?" he began blusteringly. "Why in - ?"

Then abruptly he stopped and shot an odd, puzzled glance at the White Linen Nurse, and right there before her startled eyes she saw every vestige of human expression fade out of his face as it faded out sometimes in the operating-room when in the midst of some ghastly, unforeseen emergency that left all his assistants blinking helplessly around them, his whole wonderful scientific mind seemed to break up like some chemical compound into all its meek component parts, - only to reorganize itself suddenly with some amazing explosive action that fairly knocked the breath out of all on-lookers - but was pretty apt to knock the breath into the body of the person most concerned.

When the Senior Surgeon's scientific mind had reorganized itself to meet *this* emergency he found himself infinitely more surprised at the particular type of explosion that had taken place than any other person could possibly have been.

"Miss Malgregor!" he gasped. "Speaking of preferring 'domestic service,' as you call it, - speaking of preferring domestic service to - nursing, - how would you like to consider - to consider a position of - of - well, - call it a - a position of general - heartwork - for a family of two? Myself and the Little Girl here being the 'two,' - as you understand," he added briskly.

"Why, I think it would be grand!" beamed the White Linen Nurse.

A trifle mockingly the Senior Surgeon bowed his appreciation. "Your frank and immediate - enthusiasm," he murmured, "is more, perhaps, than I had dared to expect."

"But it would be grand!" said the White Linen Nurse. Before the odd little smile in the Senior Surgeon's eyes her white forehead puckered all up with perplexity. Then with her mind still thoroughly unawakened, her heart began suddenly to pitch and lurch like a frightened horse whose rider has not even remotely sensed as yet the approach of an unwonted footfall. "What - did - you - say?" she repeated worriedly. "Just exactly what was it that you said? I guess - maybe - I didn't understand just exactly what it was that you said."

The smile in the Senior Surgeon's eyes deepened a little. "I asked you," he said, "how you would like to consider a position of 'general heartwork' in a family of two, - myself and the Little Girl here being the 'two.' 'Heartwork' was what I said. Yes, - 'Heartwork,' - not housework!"

"*Heartwork?*" faltered the White Linen Nurse. " *Heartwork?* I don't know what you mean, sir." Like two falling rose-petals her eyelids fluttered down across her affrighted eyes. "Oh, when I shut my eyes, sir, and just hear your voice, I know of course, sir, that it's some sort of a joke. But when I look right at you - I - don't know - what it is!"

"Open your eyes and keep them open then till you do find out!" suggested the Senior Surgeon bluntly.

Defiantly once again the blue eyes and the gray eyes challenged each other.

"'Heartwork' was what I said," persisted the Senior Surgeon. Palpably his narrowing eyes shut out all meaning but one definite one.

The White Linen Nurse's face went almost as blanched as her dress. "You're - you're not asking me to - marry you, sir?" she stammered.

"I suppose I am!" acknowledged the Senior Surgeon.

"Not marry you!" cried the White Linen Nurse. Distress was in her voice, - distaste, - unmitigable shock, as though the high gods themselves had fallen at her feet and splintered off into mere candy fragments.

"Oh - not *marry* you, sir?" she kept right on protesting. "Not be - *engaged*, you mean? Oh, not be *engaged* - and everything?"

"Well, why not?" snapped the Senior Surgeon.

Like a smitten flower the girl's whole body seemed to wilt

down into incalculable weariness.

"Oh - no - no! I couldn't!" she protested. "Oh, no, - really!" Appealingly she lifted her great blue eyes to his, and the blueness was all blurred with tears. "I've - I've been engaged - once - you know," she explained falteringly. "Why - I was engaged, sir, almost as soon as I was born, and I stayed engaged till two years ago. That's almost twenty years. That's a long time, sir. You don't get over it - easy." Very, very gravely she began to shake her head. "Oh - no - sir! No! Thank you - very much - but I - I just simply couldn't begin at the beginning and go all through it again! I haven't got the heart for it! I haven't got the spirit! Carvin' your initials on trees and - and gadding round to all the Sunday school picnics -"

Brutally like a boy the Senior Surgeon threw back his head in one wild hoot of joy. Infinitely more cautiously as the agonizing pang in his shoulder lulled down again he proceeded to argue the matter, but the grin in his face was even yet faintly traceable.

"Frankly, Miss Malgregor," he affirmed, "I'm infinitely more addicted to carving people than to carving trees. And as to Sunday school picnics? Well, really now - I hardly believe that you'd find my demands in that direction - excessive!"

Perplexedly the White Linen Nurse tried to stare her way through his bantering smile to his real meaning. Furiously, as she stared, the red blood came flushing back into her face.

"You don't mean for a second that you - that you love me?" she asked incredulously.

"No, I don't suppose I do!" acknowledged the Senior Surgeon with equal bluntness. "But my little kiddie here loves you!" he hastened somewhat nervously to affirm. "Oh, I'm almost sure that my little kiddie here - loves you! She needs you anyway! Let it go at that! Call it that we both - need you!"

"What you mean is -" corrected the White Linen Nurse, "that needing somebody - very badly, you've just suddenly decided that that somebody might as well be me?"

"Well - if you choose to put it - like that!" said the Senior Surgeon a bit sulkily.

"And if there hadn't been an auto accident?" argued the White Linen Nurse just out of sheer inquisitiveness, "if there hadn't been just this particular kind of an auto accident - at this particular hour - of this particular day - of this particular month - with marigolds and - everything, you probably never would have realized that you did need anybody?"

"Maybe not," admitted the Senior Surgeon.

"U - m - m," said the White Linen Nurse. "And if you'd happened to take one of the other girls to-day - instead of me, - why then I suppose you'd have felt that she was the one you really needed? And if you'd taken the Superintendent of Nurses - instead of any of us girls - you might even have felt that *she* was the one you most needed?"

With surprising agility for a man with a sprained back the Senior Surgeon wrenched himself around until he faced her quite squarely.

"Now see here, Miss Malgregor!" he growled. "For Heaven's sake listen to sense, even if you can't talk it! Here am I, a plain professional man - making you a plain professional offer. Why in thunder should you try to fuss me all up because my offer isn't couched in all the foolish, romantic, lace-paper sort of flub-dubbery that you think such an offer ought to be couched in? Eh?"

"Fuss you all up, sir?" protested the White Linen Nurse with real anxiety.

"Yes - fuss me all up!" snarled the Senior Surgeon with

increasing venom. "I'm no story-writer! I'm not trying to make up what might have happened a year from next February in a Chinese junk off the coast of – Nova Zembla - to a Methodist preacher - and a - and a militant suffragette! What I'm trying to size up is - just what's happened to you and me - to-day! For the fact remains that it is to-day! And it is you and I! And there has been an accident! And out of that accident - and everything that's gone with it - I have come out - thinking of something that I never thought of before! And there were marigolds!" he added with unexpected whimsicality. "You see I don't deny - even the marigolds!"

"Yes, sir," said the White Linen Nurse.

"Yes what?" jerked the Senior Surgeon.

Softly the White Linen Nurse's chin burrowed down a little closer against the sleeping child's tangled hair. "Why - yes - thank you very much - but I never shall love again," she said quite definitely.

"Love?" gasped the Senior Surgeon. "Why, I'm not asking you to love me!" His face was suddenly crimson. "Why, I'd hate it, if you - loved me! Why, I'd -"

"O - h - h," mumbled the White Linen Nurse in new embarrassment. Then suddenly and surprisingly her chin came tilting bravely up again. "What do you want?" she asked.

Helplessly the Senior Surgeon threw out his hands. "My goodness!" he said. "What do you suppose I want? *I want some one to take care of us!*"

Gently the White Linen Nurse shifted her shoulder to accommodate the shifting little sleepyhead on her breast.

"You can hire some one for that," she suggested with real relief.

"I was trying to hire - you!" said the Senior Surgeon quite tersely.

"Hire me?" gasped the White Linen Nurse. "Why! Why!"

Adroitly she slipped both hands under the sleeping child and delivered the little frail-fleshed, heavily ironed body into the Senior Surgeon's astonished arms.

"I - I don't want to hold her," he protested.

"She - isn't mine!" argued the White Linen Nurse.

"But I can't talk while I'm holding her!" insisted the Senior Surgeon.

"I can't listen - while I'm holding her!" persisted the White Linen Nurse.

Freely now, though cross-legged like a Turk, she jerked herself forward on the grass and sat probing up into the Senior Surgeon's face like an excited puppy trying to solve whether the gift in your up-raised hand is a lump of sugar - or a live coal.

"You're trying to hire - *me*?" she prompted him nudgingly with her voice. "Hire me - for money?"

"Oh my Lord, no!" said the Senior Surgeon. "There are plenty of people I can hire for money! But they won't stay!" he explained ruefully. "Hang it all, - they won't stay!" Above his little girl's white, pinched face his own ruddy countenance furrowed suddenly with unspeakable anxiety.

"Why, just this last year," he complained, "we've had nine different housekeepers - and thirteen nursery governesses!" Skilfully as a surgeon, but awkwardly as a father, he bent to re-adjust the weight of the little iron leg-braces. "But I tell you - no one will stay with us!" he finished hotly. "There's -

something the matter - with us! I don't seem to have money enough in the world to make anybody - stay with us!"

Very wryly, very reluctantly, at one corner of his mouth his sense of humor ignited in a feeble grin.

"So you see what I'm trying to do to you, Miss Malgregor, is to - hire you with something that will just - naturally compel you to stay!"

If the grin round his mouth strengthened a trifle, so did the anxiety in his eyes.

"For Heaven's sake, Miss Malgregor," he pleaded. "Here's a man and a house and a child all going to - rack and ruin! If you're really and truly tired of nursing - and are looking for a new job, - what's the matter with tackling us?"

"It would be a job!" admitted the White Linen Nurse demurely.

"Why, it would be a deuce-of-a-job!" confided the Senior Surgeon with no demureness whatsoever.

CHAPTER VII

Very soberly, very thoughtfully then, across the tangled, snuggling head of his own and another woman's child, he urged the torments - and the comforts of his home upon this second woman.

"What is there about my offer - that you don't like?" he demanded earnestly. "Is it the whole idea that offends you? Or just the way I put it? 'General Heartwork for a Family of Two?' What is the matter with that? Seems a bit cold to you, does it, for a real marriage proposal? Or is it that it's just a bit too ardent, perhaps, for a mere plain business proposition?"

"Yes, sir," said the White Linen Nurse.

"Yes what?" insisted the Senior Surgeon.

"Yes - *sir*," flushed the White Linen Nurse.

Very meditatively the Senior Surgeon reconsidered his phrasing. "'General Heartwork for a Family of Two'? U - m - m." Quite abruptly even the tenseness of his manner faded from him, leaving his face astonishingly quiet, astonishingly gentle. "But how else, Miss Malgregor," he queried, "How else should a widower with a child proffer marriage to a - to a young girl like yourself? Even under conditions directly antipodal to ours, such a proposition can never be a purely romantic one. Yet even under conditions as cold and business-like as ours, there's got to be some vestige of affection in it, -

some vestige at least of the *intelligence* of affection, - else what gain is there for my little girl and me over the purely mercenary domestic service that has racked us up to this time with its garish faithlessness?"

"Yes, sir," said the White Linen Nurse.

"But even if I had loved you, Miss Malgregor," explained the Senior Surgeon gravely, "my offer of marriage to you would not, I fear, have been a very great oratorical success. Materialist as I am, - cynic - scientist, - any harsh thing you choose to call me, - marriage in some freak, boyish corner of my mind, still defines itself as being the mutual sharing of a - mutually original experience. Certainly whether a first marriage be instigated in love or worldliness, - whether it eventually proves itself bliss, tragedy, or mere sickening ennui, to two people coming mutually virgin to the consummation of that marriage, the thrill of establishing publicly a man-and-woman home together is an emotion that cannot be reduplicated while life lasts."

"Yes, sir," said the White Linen Nurse.

Bleakly across the Senior Surgeon's face something gray that was not years shadowed suddenly and was gone again.

"Even so, Miss Malgregor," he argued, "even so - without any glittering romance whatsoever, no woman I believe is very grossly unhappy in any - affectional place - that she knows distinctly to be her *own* place. It's pretty much up to a man then I think, - though it tear him brain from heart, to explain to a second wife quite definitely just exactly what place it is that he is offering her in his love, - or his friendship, - or his mere desperate need. No woman can ever hope to step successfully into a second-hand home who does not know from her man's own lips the measure of her predecessor. The respect we owe the dead is a selfish thing compared to the mercy we owe the living. In my own case -"

Unconsciously the White Linen Nurse's lax shoulders quickened, and the sudden upward tilt of her chin was as frankly interrogative as a French inflection. "Yes, sir," she said.

"In my own case," said the Senior Surgeon bluntly, "in my own case, Miss Malgregor, it is no more than fair to tell you that I - did not love my wife. And my wife did not love me." Only the muscular twitch in his throat betrayed the torture that the confession cost him. "The details of that marriage are unnecessary," he continued with equal bluntness. "It is enough perhaps to say that she was the daughter of an eminent surgeon with whom I was exceedingly anxious at that time to be allied, and that our mating, urged along on both sides as it was by strong personal ambitions was one of those so-called 'marriages of convenience' which almost invariably turn out to be marriages of such dire inconvenience to the two people most concerned. For one year we lived together in a chaos of experimental acquaintanceship. For two years we lived together in increasing uncongeniality and distaste. For three years we lived together in open and acknowledged enmity. At the last, I am thankful to remember, that we had one year together again that was at least an - armed truce."

Darkly the gray shadow and the red flush chased each other once more across the man's haggard face.

"I had a theory," he said, "that possibly a child might bridge the chasm between us. My wife refuted the theory, but submitted herself reluctantly to the fact. And when she - in giving birth to - my theory, - the shock, the remorse, the regret, the merciless self-analysis that I underwent at that time almost convinced me that the whole miserable failure of our marriage lay entirely on my own shoulders." Like the stress of mid-summer the tears of sweat started suddenly on his forehead. "But I am a fair man, I hope, - even to myself, and the cooler, less-tortured judgment of the subsequent years has practically assured me that, for types as diametrically opposed as ours, such a thing as mutual happiness never could have existed."

Mechanically he bent down and smoothed a tickly lock of hair away from the little girl's eyelids.

"And the child is the living physical image of her," he stammered. "The violent hair, - the ghost-white skin, - the facile mouth, - the arrogant eyes, - staring - staring - maddeningly reproachful, persistently accusing. My own stubborn will, - my own hideous temper, - all my own ill-favored mannerisms - mocked back at me eternally in her mother's - unloved features." Mirthless as the grin of a skull, the Senior Surgeon's mouth twisted up a little at one corner. "Maybe I could have borne it better if she'd been a boy," he acknowledged grimly. "But to see all your virile - masculine vices come back at you - so sissified - in *skirts*!"

"Yes, sir," said the White Linen Nurse.

With an unmistakable gasp of relief the Senior Surgeon expanded his great chest.

"There! That's done!" he said tersely. "So much for the Past! Now for the Present! Look at us pretty keenly and judge for yourself! A man and a very little girl, - not guaranteed, - not even recommended, - offered merely 'As Is' in the honest trade-phrase of the day, - offered frankly in an open package, - accepted frankly, - if at all - 'at your own risk.' Not for an instant would I try to deceive you about us! Look at us closely, I ask, and - decide for yourself! I am forty-eight years old. I am inexcusably bad-tempered, - very quick to anger, and not, I fear, of great mercy. I am moody. I am selfish. I am most distinctly unsocial. But I am not, I believe, stingy, - nor ever intentionally unfair. My child is a cripple, - and equally bad-tempered as myself. No one but a mercenary has ever coped with her. And she shows it. We have lived alone for six years. All of our clothes, and most of our ways, need mending. I am not one to mince matters, Miss Malgregor, nor has your training, I trust, made you one from whom truths must be veiled. I am a man with all a man's needs, - mental, moral, physical. My child is a child with all a child's needs, - mental, moral, physical. Our house of life is full of cobwebs. The rooms of affection have long been closed. There will be a great deal of work to do! And it is not my intention, you see, that you should misunderstand in any conceivable way either the exact nature or the exact amount of work and worry involved. I should not want you to come to me afterwards with a whine, as other workers do, and say 'Oh, but I didn't know you would expect me to do *this!* Oh, but I hadn't any idea you would want me to do *that!* And I certainly don't see why you should expect me to give up my Thursday afternoon just because you, yourself, happened to fall down stairs in the morning and break your back!'"

Across the Senior Surgeon's face a real smile lightened suddenly.

"Really, Miss Malgregor," he affirmed, "I'm afraid there isn't much of anything that you won't be expected to do! And as to your 'Thursdays out'? Ha! If you have ever yet found a way to temper the wind of your obligations to the shorn lamb of your pleasures, you have discovered something that I myself have never yet succeeded in discovering! And as to 'wages'? Yes! I want to talk everything quite frankly! In addition to my average yearly earnings, - which are by no means small, - I have a reasonably large private fortune. Within normal limits there is no luxury I think that you cannot hope to have. Also, exclusive of the independent income which I would like to settle upon you, I should be very glad to finance for you any reasonable dreams that you may cherish concerning your family in Nova Scotia. Also, - though the offer looks small and unimportant to you now, it is liable to loom pretty large to you later, - also, I will personally guarantee to you - at some time every year, an unfettered, perfectly independent two months' holiday. So the offer stands, - my 'name and fame,' - if those mean anything to you, - financial independence, - an assured 'breathing spell' for at least two months out of twelve, - and at last but not least, - my eternal gratitude! 'General Heartwork for a Family of Two'! *There!* Have I made the task perfectly clear to you? Not everything to be done all at once, you know. But immediately where necessity urges it, - gradually as confidence inspires it, - ultimately if affection justifies it, - every womanish thing that needs to be done in a man's and a child's neglected lives? Do you understand?"

"Yes, sir," said the White Linen Nurse.

"Oh, and there's one thing more," confided the Senior Surgeon. "It's something, of course, that I ought to have told you the very first thing of all!" Nervously he glanced down at the sleeping child, and lowered his voice to a mumbling monotone. "As regards my actual morals you have naturally a right to know that I've led a pretty decent sort of life, - though I probably don't deserve any special credit for that. A man who knows enough to be a doctor isn't particularly apt to lead any other kind. Frankly, - as women rate vices I believe I have only one. What - what - I'm trying to tell you - now - is about that one." A little defiantly as to chin, a little appealingly as to eye, he emptied his heart of its last tragic secret. "Through all the male line of my family, Miss Malgregor, dipsomania runs rampant. Two of my brothers, my father, my grandfather, my great grandfather before him, have all gone down as the temperance people would say into 'drunkards' graves.' In my own case, I have chosen to compromise with the evil. Such a choice, believe me, has not been made carelessly or impulsively, but out of the agony and humiliation of - several less successful methods." Hard as a rock, his face grooved into its granite-like furrows again. "Naturally, under these existing conditions," he warned her almost threateningly, "I am not peculiarly susceptible to the mawkishly ignorant and sentimental protests of - people whose strongest passions are an appetite for - chocolate candy! For eleven months of the year," he hurried on a bit huskily, "for eleven months of the year, - eleven months, - each day reeking from dawn to dark with the driving, nerve-wracking, heart-wringing work that falls to my profession, I lead an absolutely abstemious life, touching neither wine nor liquor, nor even indeed tea or coffee. In the twelfth month, - June always, - I go way, way up into Canada, - way, way off in the woods to a little log camp I own there, -

with an Indian who has guided me thus for eighteen years. And live like a - wild man for four gorgeous, care-free, trail-tramping, salmon-fighting, - whisky-guzzling weeks. It is what your temperance friends would call a - 'spree.' To be quite frank, I suppose it is what - anybody would call a 'spree.' Then the first of July, - three or four days past the first of July perhaps, - I come out of the woods - quite tame again. A little emotionally nervous, perhaps, - a little temperishly irritable, - a little unduly sensitive about being greeted as a returned jail-bird, - but most miraculously purged of all morbid craving for liquor, and with every digital muscle as coolly steady as yours, and every conscious mental process clamoring cleanly for its own work again."

Furtively under his glowering brows he stopped and searched the White Linen Nurse's imperturbable face. "It's an - established custom, you understand," he rewarned her. "I'm not advocating it, you understand, - I'm not defending it. I'm simply calling your attention to the fact that it is an established custom. If you decide to come to us, I - I couldn't, you know, at forty-eight - begin all over again to - to have some one waiting for me on the top step the first of July to tell me - what a low beast I am - till I go down the steps again - the following June."

"No, of course not," conceded the White Linen Nurse. Blandly she lifted her lovely eyes to his. "Father's like that!" she confided amiably. "Once a year, - just Easter Sunday only, - he always buys him a brand new suit of clothes and goes to church. And it does something to him, - I don't know exactly what, but Easter afternoon he always gets drunk, - oh mad, fighting drunk is what I mean, and goes out and tries to tear up the whole county." Worriedly two black thoughts puckered between her eyebrows. "And always," she said, "he makes Mother and me go up to Halifax beforehand to pick out the suit for him. It's pretty hard sometimes," she said, "to find anything dressy enough for the morning, that's serviceable enough for the afternoon."

"Eh?" jerked the Senior Surgeon. Then suddenly he began to smile again like a stormy sky from which the last cloud has just been cleared. "Well, it's all right then, is it? You'll take us?" he asked brightly.

"Oh, no!" said the White Linen Nurse. "Oh, no, sir! Oh, no indeed, sir!" Quite perceptibly she jerked her way backward a little on the grass. "Thank you very much!" she persisted courteously. "It's been very interesting! I thank you very much for telling me, but -"

"But what?" snapped the Senior Surgeon.

"But it's too quick," said the White Linen Nurse. "No man could tell like that - just between one eye-wink and another what he wanted about anything, - let alone marrying a perfect stranger."

Instantly the Senior Surgeon bridled. "I assure you, my dear young lady," he retorted, "that I am entirely and completely accustomed to deciding between 'one wink and another' just exactly what it is that I want. Indeed, I assure you that there are a good many people living to-day who wouldn't be living, if it had taken me even as long as a wink and three-quarters to make up my mind!"

"Yes, I know, sir," acknowledged the White Linen Nurse. "Yes, of course, sir," she acquiesced with most commendable humility. "But all the same, sir, I couldn't do it!" she persisted with inflexible positiveness. "Why, I haven't enough education," she confessed quite shamelessly.

"You had enough, I notice, to get into the hospital," drawled the Senior Surgeon a bit grumpily. "And that's quite as much as most people have, I assure you! 'A High School education or its equivalent,' - that is the hospital requirement, I believe?" he questioned tartly.

"'A High School education or its - equivocation' is what we

girls call it," confessed the White Linen Nurse demurely. "But even so, sir," she pleaded, "it isn't just my lack of education! It's my brains! I tell you, sir, I haven't got enough brains to do what you suggest!"

"I don't mean at all to belittle your brains," grinned the Senior Surgeon in spite of himself. "Oh, not at all, Miss Malgregor! But you see it isn't especially brains that I'm looking for! Really what I need most," he acknowledged frankly, "is an extra pair of hands to go with the - brains I already possess!"

"Yes, I know, sir," persisted the White Linen Nurse. "Yes, of course, sir," she conceded. "Yes, of course, sir, my hands work - awfully - well - with your face. But all the same," she kindled suddenly, "all the same, sir, I can't! I won't! I tell you sir, I won't! Why, I'm not in your world, sir! Why, I'm not in your class! Why - my folks aren't like your folks! Oh, we're just as good as you - of course - but we aren't as nice! Oh, we're not nice at all! Really and truly we're not!" Desperately through her mind she rummaged up and down for some one conclusive fact that would close this torturing argument for all time. "Why - my father - eats with his knife," she asserted triumphantly.

"Would he be apt to eat with mine?" asked the Senior Surgeon with extravagant gravity.

Precipitously the White Linen Nurse jumped to the defense of her father's intrinsic honor. "Oh, no!" she denied with some vehemence. "Father's never cheeky like that! Father's simple sometimes, - plain, I mean. Or he might be a bit sharp. But, oh, I'm sure he'd never be - cheeky! Oh, no, sir! No!"

"Oh, very well then," grinned the Senior Surgeon. "We can consider everything all comfortably settled then I suppose?"

"No, we can't!" screamed the White Linen Nurse. A little awkwardly with cramped limbs she struggled partly upward from the grass and knelt there defying the Senior Surgeon from her temporarily superior height. "No, we can't!" she reiterated wildly. "I tell you I can't, sir! I won't! I won't! I've been engaged once and it's enough! I tell you, sir, I'm all engaged out!"

"What's become of the man you were engaged to?" quizzed the Senior Surgeon sharply.

"Why - he's married!" said the White Linen Nurse. "And they've got a kid!" she added tempestuously.

"Good! I'm glad of it!" smiled the Senior Surgeon quite amazingly. "Now he surely won't bother us any more."

"But I was engaged so long!" protested the White Linen Nurse. "Almost ever since I was born, I said. It's too long. You don't get over it!"

"He got over it," remarked the Senior Surgeon laconically.

"Y-e-s," admitted the White Linen Nurse. "But I tell you it doesn't seem decent. Not after being engaged - twenty years!" With a little helpless gesture of appeal she threw out her hands. "Oh, can't I make you understand, sir?"

"Why, of course, I understand," said the Senior Surgeon briskly. "You mean that you and John -"

"His name was 'Joe,'" corrected the White Linen Nurse.

With astonishing amiability the Senior Surgeon acknowledged the correction. "You mean," he said, "you mean that you and - Joe - have been cradled together so familiarly all your babyhood that on your wedding night you could most naturally have said 'Let me see - Joe, - it's two pillows that you always have, isn't it? And a double-fold of blanket at the foot?' You mean that you and Joe have been washed and scrubbed together so familiarly all your young childhood that you could identify Joe's headless body twenty years hence by the kerosene-lamp scar across his back? You mean that you and Joe have played house together so familiarly all your young tin-dish days that even your rag dolls called Joe 'Father'? You mean that since your earliest memory, - until a year or so ago, - Life has never once been just You and Life, but always You and Life and Joe? You and Spring and Joe, - You and Summer and Joe, - You and Autumn and Joe, - You and Winter and Joe, - till every conscious nerve in your body has been so everlastingly Joed with Joe's Joeness that you don't believe there 's any experience left in life powerful enough to eradicate that original impression? Eh?"

"Yes, sir," flushed the White Linen Nurse.

"Good! I'm glad of it!" snapped the Senior Surgeon. "It doesn't make you seem quite so alarmingly innocent and remote for a widower to offer marriage to. Good, I say! I'm glad of it!"

"Even so - I don't want to," said the White Linen Nurse. "Thank you very much, sir! But even so, I don't want to."

"Would you marry - Joe - now if he were suddenly free and wanted you?" asked the Senior Surgeon bluntly.

"Oh, my Lord, no!" said the White Linen Nurse.

"Other men are pretty sure to want you," admonished the Senior Surgeon. "Have you made up your mind - definitely that you'll never marry anybody?"

"N - o, not exactly," confessed the White Linen Nurse.

An odd flicker twitched across the Senior Surgeon's face like a sob in the brain.

"What's your first name, Miss Malgregor?" he asked a bit huskily.

"Rae," she told him with some surprise.

The Senior Surgeon's eyes narrowed suddenly again.

"Damn it all, Rae," he said, "*I - want you!*"

Precipitously the White Linen Nurse scrambled to her feet. "If you don't mind, sir," she cried, "I'll run down to the brook and get myself a drink of water!"

Impishly like a child, muscularly like a man, the Senior Surgeon clutched out at the flapping corner of her coat.

"No you don't!" he laughed, "till you've given me my definite answer - yes or no!"

Breathlessly the White Linen Nurse spun round in her tracks. Her breast was heaving with ill-suppressed sobs. Her eyes were blurred with tears. "You've no business - to hurry me so!" she protested passionately. "It isn't fair! - It isn't kind!"

Sluggishly in the Senior Surgeon's jolted arms the Little Girl woke from her feverish nap and peered up perplexedly through the gray dusk into her father's face.

"Where's - my kitty?" she asked hazily.

"Eh?" jerked the Senior Surgeon.

Harshly the little iron leg-braces clanked together.

In an instant the White Linen Nurse was on her knees in the grass. "You don't hold her right, sir!" she expostulated. Deftly with little soft, darting touches, interrupted only by rubbing her knuckles into her own tears, she reached out and eased successively the bruise of a buckle or the dragging weight on a little cramped hip.

Still drowsily, still hazily, with little smacking gasps and gulping swallows, the child worried her way back again into consciousness.

"All the birds *were* there, Father," she droned forth feebly from her sweltering mink-fur nest.

All the birds *were* there
With yellow feathers instead of - hair,
And bumble bees - and bumble bees -
And bumble bees? - And bumble bees - ?

Frenziedly she began to burrow the back of her head into her Father's shoulder. "And bumble bees? - And bumble bees - ?"

"Oh, for Heaven's sake - 'buzzed' in the trees!" interpolated the Senior Surgeon.

Rigidly from head to foot the little body in his arms stiffened suddenly. As one who saw the supreme achievement of a lifetime swept away by some one careless joggle of an infinitesimal part, the Little Girl stared up agonizingly into her father's face. "Oh, I don't think - 'buzzed' was the word!" she began convulsively. "Oh, I don't think - !"

Startlingly through the twilight the Senior Surgeon felt the White Linen Nurse's rose-red lips come smack against his ear.

"Darn you! Can't you say 'crocheted' in the trees?" sobbed the White Linen Nurse.

Grotesquely for an instant the Senior Surgeon's eyes and the White Linen Nurse's eyes glared at each other in frank antagonism.

Then suddenly the Senior Surgeon burst out laughing. "Oh, very well!" he surrendered. "'Crocheted in the trees'!"

Precipitously the White Linen Nurse sank back on her heels and began to clap her hands.

"Oh, now I will! Now I will!" she cried exultantly.

"Will what?" frowned the Senior Surgeon.

Abruptly the White Linen Nurse stopped clapping her hands and began to wring them nervously in her lap instead. "Why - will - will!" she confessed demurely.

"Oh!" jumped the Senior Surgeon. "*Oh!*" Then equally jerkily he began to pucker his eyebrows. "But for Heaven's sake - what's the 'crocheted in the trees' got to do with it?" he asked perplexedly.

"Nothing much," mused the White Linen Nurse very softly. With sudden alertness she turned her curly blonde head towards the road. "There's somebody coming!" she said. "I hear a team!"

Overcome by a bashfulness that tried to escape in jocosity, the Senior Surgeon gave an odd little choking chuckle.

"Well, I never thought I should marry a - trained nurse!" he acknowledged with somewhat hectic blitheness.

Impulsively the White Linen Nurse reached for her watch and lifted it close to her twilight-blinded eyes. A sense of ineffable peace crept suddenly over her.

"You won't, sir!" she said amiably.

"It's twenty minutes of nine, now. And the graduation was at eight!"

CHAPTER VIII

For any real adventure except dying, June is certainly a most auspicious month.

Indeed it was on the very first rain-green, rose-red morning of June that the White Linen Nurse sallied forth upon her extremely hazardous adventure of marrying the Senior Surgeon and his naughty little crippled daughter.

The wedding was at noon in some kind of a gray granite church. And the Senior Surgeon was there, of course, - and the necessary witnesses. But the Little Crippled Girl never turned up at all, owing - it proved later, - to a more than usually violent wrangle with whomever dressed her, concerning the general advisability of sporting turquoise-colored stockings with her brightest little purple dress.

The Senior Surgeon's stockings, if you really care to know, were gray. And the Senior Surgeon's suit was gray. And he looked altogether very huge and distinguished, - and no more strikingly unhappy than any bridegroom looks in a gray granite church.

And the White Linen Nurse, - no longer now truly a White Linen Nurse but just an ordinary, every-day, silk-and-cloth lady of any color she chose, wore something rather coat-y and grand and bluish, and was distractingly pretty of course but most essentially unfamiliar, - and just a tiny bit awkward and bony-wristed looking, - as even an Admiral is apt to be on his first day out of uniform.

Then as soon as the wedding ceremony was over, the bride and groom went to a wonderful green and gold café all built of marble and lined with music, and had a little lunch. What I really mean, of course, is that they had a very large lunch, but didn't eat any of it!

Then in a taxi-cab, just exactly like any other taxi-cab, the White Linen Nurse drove home alone to the Senior Surgeon's great, gloomy house to find her brand new step-daughter still screaming over the turquoise colored stockings.

And the Senior Surgeon in a Canadian-bound train, just exactly like any other Canadian-bound train, started off alone, - as usual, on his annual June "spree."

Please don't think for a moment that it was the Senior Surgeon who was responsible for the general eccentricities of this amazing wedding day. No indeed! The Senior Surgeon didn't *want* to be married the first day of June! He *said* he didn't! He *growled* he didn't! He *snarled* he didn't! He *swore* he didn't! And when he finished saying and growling and snarling and swearing, - and looked up at the White Linen Nurse for a confirmation of his opinion, the White Linen Nurse smiled perfectly amiably and said, "Yes, sir!"

Then the Senior Surgeon gave a great gasp of relief and announced resonantly, "Well, it's all settled then? We'll be married some time in July, - after I get home from Canada?" And when the White Linen Nurse kept on smiling perfectly amiably and said, "Oh, no, sir! Oh, no, thank you, sir! It wouldn't seem exactly legal to me to be married any other month but June!" Then the Senior Surgeon went absolutely dumb with rage that this mere chit of a girl, - and a trained nurse, too, - should dare to thwart his personal and professional convenience. But the White Linen Nurse just drooped her pretty blonde head and blushed and blushed and blushed and said, "I was only marrying you, sir, to -

accommodate you - sir, - and if June doesn't accommodate you - I'd rather go to Japan with that monoideic somnambulism case. It's very interesting. And it sails June second." Then "Oh, Hell with the 'monoideic somnambulism case'!" the Senior Surgeon would protest.

Really it took the Senior Surgeon quite a long while to work out the three special arguments that should best protect him, he thought, from the horridly embarrassing idea of being married in June.

"But you can't get ready so soon!" he suggested at last with real triumph. "You've no idea how long it takes a girl to get ready to be married! There are so many people she has to tell, - and everything!"

"There's never but two that she's got to tell - or bust!" conceded the White Linen Nurse with perfect candor. "Just the woman she loves the most - and the woman she hates the worst. I'll write my mother to-morrow. But I told the Superintendent of Nurses yesterday."

"The deuce you did!" snapped the Senior Surgeon.

Almost caressingly the White Linen Nurse lifted her big blue eyes to his. "Yes, sir," she said, "and she looked as sick as a young undertaker. I can't imagine what ailed her."

"Eh?" choked the Senior Surgeon. "But the house now," he hastened to contend. "The house now needs a lot of fixing over! It's all run down! It's all - everything! We never in the world could get it into shape by the first of June! For Heaven's sake, now that we've got money enough to make it right, let's go slow and make it perfectly right!"

A little nervously the White Linen Nurse began to fumble through the pages of her memorandum book. "I've always had money enough to 'go slow and make things perfectly right,'" she confided a bit wistfully. "Never in all my life have I had a pair of boots that weren't guaranteed, or a dress that wouldn't wash, or a hat that wasn't worth at least three re-pressings. What I was hoping for now, sir, was that I was going to have enough money so that I could go fast and make things wrong if I wanted to, - so that I could afford to take chances, I mean. Here's this wall-paper now," - tragically she pointed to some figuring in her note-book - "it's got peacocks on it - life size - in a queen's garden - and I wanted it for the dining-room. Maybe it would fade! Maybe we'd get tired of it! Maybe it would poison us! Slam it on one week - and slash it off the next! I wanted it just because I wanted it, sir! I thought maybe - while you were way off in Canada -"

Eagerly the Senior Surgeon jerked his chair a little nearer to his - fiancée's.

"Now, my dear girl," he said. "That's just what I want to explain! That's just what I want to explain! Just what I want to explain! To - er - explain!" he continued a bit falteringly.

"Yes, sir," said the White Linen Nurse.

Very deliberately the Senior Surgeon removed a fleck of dust from one of his cuffs.

"All this talk of yours - about wanting to be married the same day I start off on my - Canadian trip!" he contended. "Why, it's all damned nonsense!"

"Yes, sir," said the White Linen Nurse.

Very conscientiously the Senior Surgeon began to search for a fleck of dust on his other cuff.

"Why my - my dear girl," he persisted. "It's absurd! It's outrageous! Why people would - would hoot at us! Why they'd think - !"

"Yes, sir," said the White Linen Nurse.

"Why, my dear girl," sweated the Senior Surgeon. "Even though you and I understand perfectly well the purely formal, business-like conditions of our marriage, we must at least for sheer decency's sake keep up a certain semblance of marital conventionality - before the world! Why, if we were married at noon the first day of June - as you suggest, - and I should go right off alone as usual - on my Canadian trip - and you should come back alone to the house - why, people would think - would think that I didn't care anything about you!"

"But you don't," said the White Linen Nurse serenely.

"Why, they'd think," choked the Senior Surgeon. "They'd think you were trying your - darndest - to get rid of me!"

"I am," said the White Linen Nurse complacently.

With a muttered ejaculation the Senior Surgeon jumped to his feet and stood glaring down at her.

Quite ingenuously the White Linen Nurse met and parried the glare.

"A gentleman - and a red-haired kiddie - and a great walloping house - all at once! It's too much!" she confided genially. "Thank you just the same, but I'd rather take them gradually. First of all, sir, you see, I've got to teach the little kiddie to like me! And then there's a green-tiled paper with floppity sea gulls on it - that I want to try for the bath-room! And - and -" Ecstatically she clapped her hands together. "Oh, sir! There are such loads and loads of experiments I want to try while you are off on your spree!"

"S - h - h!" cried the Senior Surgeon. His face was suddenly blanched, - his mouth, twitching like the mouth of one stricken with almost insupportable pain. "For God's sake, Miss Malgregor!" he pleaded, "can't you call it my - Canadian trip?"

Wider and wider the White Linen Nurse opened her big blue

eyes at him.

"But it is a 'spree,' sir!" she attested resolutely. "And my father says -" Still resolutely her young mouth curved to its original assertion, but from under her heavy-shadowing eyelashes a little blue smile crept softly out. "When my father's got a lame trotting horse, sir, that he's trying to shuck off his hands," she faltered, "he doesn't ever go round mournful-like with his head hanging - telling folks about his wonderful trotter that's just 'the littlest, teeniest, tiniest bit - lame.' Oh no! What father does is to call up every one he knows within twenty miles and tell 'em, 'Say Tom, - Bill, - Harry,' - or whatever his name is - 'what in the deuce do you suppose I've got over here in my barn? A lame horse - that wants to trot! Lamer than the deuce, you know! But can do a mile in 2.40.'" Faintly the little blue smile quickened again in the White Linen Nurse's eyes. "And the barn will be full of men in half an hour!" she said. "Somehow nobody wants a trotter that's lame! But almost anybody seems willing to risk a lame horse - that's plucky enough to trot!"

"What's the 'lame trotting horse' got to do with - me?" snarled the Senior Surgeon incisively.

Darkly the White Linen Nurse's lashes fringed down across her cheeks.

"Nothing much," she said, "Only -"

"Only what?" demanded the Senior Surgeon. A little more roughly than he realized he stooped down and took the White Linen Nurse by her shoulders, and jerked her sharply round to the light. "Only *what?*" he insisted peremptorily.

Almost plaintively she lifted her eyes to his. "Only - my father says," she confided obediently, "my father says if you've got a worse foot - for Heaven's sake put it forward - and get it over with!

"So - I've *got* to call it a 'spree'!" smiled the White Linen Nurse. "'Cause when I think of marrying a - *surgeon* - that goes off and gets drunk every June - it - it scares me almost to my death! But -" Abruptly the red smile faded from her lips, the blue smile from her eyes. "But - when I think of marrying a - June drunk - that's got the grit to pull up absolutely straight as a die and be a *surgeon* - all the other 'leven months in the year -" Dartingly she bent down and kissed the Senior Surgeon's astonished wrist. "Oh, then I think you're perfectly *grand*!" she sobbed.

Awkwardly the Senior Surgeon pulled away and began to pace the floor.

"You're a - good little girl, Rae Malgregor," he mumbled huskily. "A good little girl. I truly believe you're the kind that will - see me through." Poignantly in his eyes humiliation overwhelmed the mist. Perversely in its turn resentment overtook the humiliation. "But I won't be married in June!" he reasserted bombastically. "I won't! I won't! I won't! I tell you I positively refuse to have a lot of damn fools speculating about my private affairs! Wondering why I didn't take you! Wondering why I didn't stay home with you! I tell you I won't! I simply won't!"

"Yes, sir," stammered the White Linen Nurse.

With a real gasp of relief the Senior Surgeon stopped his eternal pacing of the floor.

"Bully for you!" he said. "You mean then we'll be married some time in July after I get back from my - trip?"

"Oh, no, sir," stammered the White Linen Nurse.

"But Great Heavens!" shouted the Senior Surgeon.

"Yes, sir," the White Linen Nurse began all over again. Dreamily planning out her wedding gown, her lips without the slightest conscious effort on her part were already curving into shape for her alternate "No, sir."

"You're an idiot!" snapped the Senior Surgeon.

A little reproachfully the White Linen Nurse came frowning out of her reverie. "Would it do just as well for traveling, do you think?" she asked, with real concern.

"Eh? What?" said the Senior Surgeon.

"I mean - does Japan spot?" queried the White Linen Nurse. "Would it spot a serge, I mean?"

"Oh, Hell with Japan!" jerked the Senior Surgeon.

"Yes, sir," said the White Linen Nurse.

Now perhaps you will understand just exactly how it happened that the Senior Surgeon and the White Linen Nurse *were* married on the first day of June, and just exactly how it happened that the Senior Surgeon went off alone as usual on his Canadian trip, and just exactly how it happened that the White Linen Nurse came home alone to the Senior Surgeon's great, gloomy house, to find her brand new step-daughter still screaming over the turquoise-colored stockings. Everything now is perfectly comfortably explained except the turquoise-colored stockings. Nobody could explain the turquoise-colored stockings!

But even a little child could explain the ensuing June! Oh, June was perfectly wonderful that year! Bud, blossom, bird-song, breeze, - rioting headlong through the Land. Warm days sweet and lush as a gre en-housevapor! Crisp nights faintly metallic like the scent of stars! Hurdy-gurdies romping tunefully on every street-corner! Even the Ash-Man flushing frankly pink across his dusty cheek-bones!

Like two fairies who had sublet a giant's cave the White Linen

Nurse and the Little Crippled Girl turned themselves loose upon the Senior Surgeon's gloomy old house.

It certainly was a gloomy old house, but handsome withal, - square and brown and substantial, and most generously gardened within high brick walls. Except for dusting the lilac bushes with the hose, and weeding a few rusty leaves out of the privet hedge, and tacking up three or four scraggly sprays of English ivy, and re-greening one or two bay-tree boxes, there was really nothing much to do to the garden. But the house? Oh ye gods! All day long from morning till night, - but most particularly from the back door to the barn, sweating workmen scuttled back and forth till nary a guilty piece of black walnut furniture had escaped. All day long from morning till night, - but most particularly from ceilings to floors, sweltering workmen scurried up and down step-ladders stripping dingy papers from dingier plasterings.

When the White Linen Nurse wasn't busy renovating the big house - or the little step-daughter, she was writing to the Senior Surgeon. She wrote twice.

"Dear Dr. Faber," the first letter said.

* * * * *

DEAR DR. FABER,

How do you do? Thank you very much, for saying you didn't care what in thunder I did to the house. It looks *sweet.* I've put white fluttery muslin curtains most everywhere. And you've got a new solid-gold-looking bed in your room. And the Kiddie and I have fixed up the most scrumptious light blue suite for ourselves in the ell. Pink was wrong for the front hall, but it cost me only $29.00 to find out. And now that's settled for all time.

I am very, very, very, very busy. Something strange and new happens every day. Yesterday it was three ladies and a plumber. One of the ladies was just selling soap, but I didn't buy any. It was horrid soap. The other two were calling ladies, - a silk one and a velvet one. The silk one tried to be nasty to me. Right to my face she told me I was more of a lady than she had dared to hope. And I told her I was sorry for that as you'd had one "lady" and it didn't work. Was that all right? But the other lady was nice. And I took her out in the kitchen with me while I was painting the woodwork, and right there in her white kid gloves she laughed and showed me how to mix the paint pearl gray. *she* was nice. It was your sister-in-law.

I like being married, Dr. Faber. I like it lots better than I thought I would. It's fun being the biggest person in the house. Respectfully yours, RAE MALGREGOR, - AS WAS.

P.S. Oh, I hope it wasn't wrong, but in your ulster pocket, when I went to put it away, I found a bottle of something that smelt as though it had been forgotten. - I threw it out.

* * * * *

It was this letter that drew the only definite message from the itinerant bridegroom.

"Kindly refrain from rummaging in my ulster pockets," wrote the Senior Surgeon quite briefly. "The 'thing' you threw out happened to be the cerebellum and medulla of an extremely eminent English Theologian!"

"Even so, - it was sour," telegraphed the White Linen Nurse in a perfect agony of remorse and humiliation.

The telegram took an Indian with a birch canoe two days to deliver, and cost the Senior Surgeon twelve dollars. Just impulsively the Senior Surgeon decided to make no further comments on domestic affairs, - at that particular range.

Very fortunately for this impulse the White Linen Nurse's second letter concerned itself almost entirely with matters quite extraneous to the home.

"Dear Dr. Faber," the second letter ran.

* * * * *

DEAR DR. FABER,

Somehow I don't seem to care so much just now about being the biggest person in the house. Something awful has happened. Zillah Forsyth is dead. Really dead, I mean. And she died in great heroism. You remember Zillah Forsyth, don't you? She was one of my room-mates, - not the gooder one, you know, - not the swell, - that was Helene Churchill. But Zillah? Oh you know! Zillah was the one you sent out on that Fractured Elbow case. It was a Yale student, you remember? And there was some trouble about kissing, - and she got sent home? And now everybody's crying because Zillah *can't* kiss anybody any more! Isn't everything the limit? Well, it wasn't a fractured Yale student she got sent out on this time. If it had been, she might have been living yet. What they sent her out on this time was a Senile Dementia, - an old lady more than eighty years old. And they were in a sanitarium or something like that. And there was a fire in the night. And the old lady just up and positively refused to escape. And Zillah had to push her and shove her and yank her and carry her - out the window - along the gutters - round the chimneys. And the old lady bit Zillah right through the hand, - but Zillah wouldn't let go. And the old lady tried to drown Zillah under a bursted water tank, - but Zillah wouldn't let go. And everybody hollered to Zillah to cut loose and save herself, - but Zillah wouldn't let go. And a wall fell, and everything, and oh, it was awful, - but Zillah never let go. And the old lady that wasn't any good to any one, - not even herself, got saved of course. But Zillah? Oh, Zillah got hurt bad, sir! We saw her at the hospital, Helene and I. She sent for us about something. Oh, it was awful! Not a thing about her that you'd know except just her great solemn eyes mooning out at you through a gob of white cotton, and her red mouth lipping sort of twitchy at the edge of a bandage. Oh it was awful! But Zillah didn't seem to care so much. There was a new Interne there, - a Japanese, and I guess she was sort of taken with him. "But my God, Zillah," I said, "*your* life was worth more than that old dame's!"

"Shut your noise!" says Zillah. "It was my job. And there's no kick coming." Helene burst right out crying, she did. "Shut *your* noise, too!" says Zillah, just as cool as you please. "Bah! There's other lives and other chances!"

"Oh, you do believe that now?" cries Helene. "Oh, you do believe that now, - what the Bible promises you?" That was when Zillah shrugged her shoulders so funny, - the little way she had. Gee, but her eyes were big! "I don't pretend to know - what - your old Bible says," she choked. "It was - the Yale feller - who was tellin' me."

That's all, Dr. Faber. It was her shrugging her shoulders so funny that brought on the hemorrhage.

Oh, we had an awful time, sir, going home in the carriage, - Helene and I. We both cried, of course, because Zillah was dead, but after we got through crying for that, Helene kept right on crying because she couldn't understand why a brave girl like Zillah *had* to be dead. Gee! But Helene takes things hard. Ladies do, I guess.

I hope you're having a pleasant spree.

Oh, I forgot to tell you that one of the wall-paperers is living here at the house with us just now. We use him so much it's truly a good deal more convenient. And he's a real nice young fellow, and he plays the piano finely, and he comes from up my way. And it seemed more neighborly anyway. It's so large in the house at night, just now, and so creaky in the garden.

With kindest regards, good-by for now, from RAE.

P.S.

Don't tell your guide or *any one!* But Helene sent Zillah's mother a check for fifteen hundred dollars. I saw it with my own eyes. And all Zillah asked for that day was just a little blue serge suit. It seems she'd promised her kid sister a little blue serge suit for July. And it sort of worried her.

Helene sent the little blue serge suit too! And a hat! The hat had bluebells on it. Do you think when you come home - if I haven't spent too much money on wall-papers - that I could have a blue hat with bluebells on it? Excuse me for bothering you - but you forgot to leave me enough money.

* * * * *

It was some indefinite, pleasant time on Thursday, the twenty-fifth of June, that the Senior Surgeon received this second letter.

It was Friday the twenty-sixth of June, exactly at dawn, that the Senior Surgeon started homeward.

Nobody looks very well in the dawn. Certainly the Senior Surgeon didn't. Heavily as a man wading through a bog of dreams, he stumbled out of his cabin into the morning. Under his drowsy, brooding eyes appalling shadows circled. Behind his sunburn, - deeper than his tan, something sinister and uncanny lurked wanly like the pallor of a soul.

Yet the Senior Surgeon had been most blamelessly abed and asleep since griddle-cake time the previous evening.

Only the mountains and the forest and the lake had been out all night. For seventy miles of Canadian wilderness only the mountains and the forest and the lake stood actually convicted of having been out all night. Dank and white with its vaporous vigil the listless lake kindled wanly to the new day's breeze. Blue with cold a precipitous mountain peak lurched craggedly home through a rift in the fog. Drenched with mist, bedraggled with dew, a green-feathered pine tree lay guzzling insatiably at a leaf-brown pool. Monotonous as a sob the waiting birch canoe slosh-sloshed against the beach.

There was no romantic smell of red roses in this June landscape. Just tobacco smoke, and the faint reminiscent fragrance of fried trout, and the mournful, sizzling, pungent consciousness of a camp-fire quenched for a whole year with a tinful of wet coffee grounds.

Gliding out cautiously into the lake as though the mere splash of a paddle might shatter the whole glassy surface, the Indian Guide propounded the question that was uppermost in his mind.

"Cutting your trip a bit short this year, - ain't you, Boss?" quizzed the Indian guide.

Out from his muffling mackinaw collar the Senior Surgeon parried the question with an amazingly novel sense of embarrassment.

"Oh, I don't know," he answered with studied lightness. "There are one or two things at home that are bothering me a little."

"A woman, eh?" said the Indian Guide laconically.

"A woman?" thundered the Senior Surgeon. "A - woman? Oh, ye gods! No! It's wall paper!"

Then suddenly and unexpectedly in the midst of his passionate refutation the Senior Surgeon burst out laughing, - boisterously, hilariously like a crazy school-boy. Bluntly from an overhanging ledge of rock the echo of his laugh came mocking back at him. Down from some unvisioned mountain fastness the echo of that echo came wafting faintly to him.

The Senior Surgeon's laugh was made of teeth and tongue and palate and a purely convulsive physical impulse. But the echo's laugh was a phantasy of mist and dawn and inestimable balsam-scented spaces where little green ferns and little brown beasties and soft-breasted birdlings frolicked eternally in pristine sweetness.

Seven miles further down the lake, at the beginning of the rapids, the Indian Guide spoke again. Racking the canoe between two rocks, - paddling, panting, pushing, sweating, the Indian Guide lifted his voice high, - piercing, above the swirling roar of waters.

"Eh, Boss!" shouted the Indian Guide. "I ain't never heard you laugh before!"

Neither man spoke again more than once or twice during the long, strenuous hours that were left to them.

The Indian Guide was very busy in his stolid mind trying to figure out just how many rows of potatoes could be planted fruitfully between his front door and his cow-shed. I don't know what the Senior Surgeon was trying to figure out.

It was just four days later from a rolling, musty-cushioned hack that the Senior Surgeon disembarked at his own front gate.

Even though a man likes home no better than he likes - tea, few men would deny the soothing effect of home at the end of a long fussy railroad journey. Five o'clock, also, of a late June afternoon is a peculiarly wonderful time to be arriving home, - especially if that home has a garden around it so that you are thereby not rushed precipitously upon the house itself, as upon a cup without a saucer, but can toy visually with the whole effect before you quench your thirst with the actual draught.

Very, very deliberately, with his clumsy rod-case in one hand, and his heavy grip in the other, the Senior Surgeon started up the long, broad gravel path to the house. For a man walking as slow as he was, his heart was beating most extraordinarily fast. He was not accustomed to heart-palpitation. The symptom worried him a trifle. Incidentally also his lungs felt strangely stifled with the scent of June. Close at his right an effulgent white and gold syringa bush flaunted its cloying sweetness into his senses. Close at his left a riotous bloom of phlox clamored red-blue-purple-lavender-pink into his dazzled vision. Multi-colored pansies tiptoed velvet-footed across the grass. In soft murky mystery a flame-tinted smoke tree loomed up here and there like a faintly rouged ghost. Over everything, under everything, through everything, lurked a certain strange, novel, vibrating consciousness of *occupancy*. Bees in the rose bushes! Bobolinks in the trees! A woman's work-basket in the curve of the hammock! A doll's tea set sprawling cheerfully in the middle of the broad gravel path!

It was not until the Senior Surgeon had actually stepped into the tiny cream pitcher that he noticed the presence of the doll's tea set.

It was what the Senior Surgeon said as he stepped out of the cream pitcher that summoned the amazing apparition from a ragged green hole in the privet hedge. Startlingly white, startlingly professional, - dress, cap, apron and all, - a miniature white linen nurse sprang suddenly out at him like a tricky dwarf in a moving picture show. Just at that particular moment the Senior Surgeon's nerves were in no condition to wrestle with apparitions. Simultaneously as the clumsy rod-case dropped from his hand, the expression of enthusiasm dropped from the face of the miniature white linen nurse.

"Oh, dear - oh, dear - oh, dear! Have *you* come home?" wailed the familiar, shrill little voice.

Sheepishly the Senior Surgeon picked up his rod-case. The noises in his head were crashing like cracked bells. Desperately with a boisterous irritability he sought to cover also the lurching pound-pound-pound of his heart.

"What in Hell are you rigged out like that for?" he demanded stormily.

With equal storminess the Little Girl protested the question.

"Peach said I could!" she attested passionately. "Peach said I could! She did! She did! I tell you I didn't want her to marry us - that day! I was afraid, I was! I cried, I did! I had a convulsion! They thought it was stockings! So Peach said if it would make me feel any gooderer, I could be the cruel new step-mother. And she'd be the unloved offspring - with her hair braided all yellow fluffikins down her back!"

"Where *is* - Miss Malgregor?" asked the Senior Surgeon sharply.

Irrelevantly the Little Girl sank down on the gravel walk and began to gather up her scattered dishes.

"And it's fun to go to bed - now," she confided amiably. "'Cause every night I put Peach to bed at eight o'clock and she's so naughty always I have to stay with her! And then all of a sudden it's morning - like going through a black room without knowing it!"

"I said - where *is* Miss Malgregor?" repeated the Senior Surgeon with increasing sharpness.

Thriftily the Little Girl bent down to lap a bubble of cream from the broken pitcher.

"Oh, she's out in the summer house with the Wall Paper Man," she mumbled indifferently.

CHAPTER IX

Altogether jerkily the Senior Surgeon started up the walk for his own perfectly formal and respectable brown stone mansion. Deep down in his lurching heart he felt a sudden most inordinate desire to reach that brown stone mansion just as quickly as possible. But abruptly even to himself he swerved off instead at the yellow sassafras tree and plunged quite wildly through a mass of broken sods towards the rickety, no-account cedar summer house.

Startled by the crackle and thud of his approach the two young figures in the summer house jumped precipitously to their feet, and limply untwining their arms from each other's necks stood surveying the Senior Surgeon in unspeakable consternation, - the White Linen Nurse and a blue overalled lad most unconscionably mated in radiant youth and agonized confusion.

"Oh, my Lord, Sir!" gasped the White Linen Nurse. "Oh, my Lord, Sir! I wasn't looking for *you* - for another week!"

"Evidently not!" said the Senior Surgeon incisively. "This is the second time this evening that I've been led to infer that my home-coming was distinctly inopportune!"

Very slowly, very methodically, he put down first his precious rod-case and then his grip. His brain seemed fairly foaming with blood and confusion. Along the swelling veins of his arms a dozen primitive instincts went surging to his fists.

Then quite brazenly before his eyes the White Linen Nurse reached out and took the lad's hand again.

"Oh, forgive me, Dr. Faber!" she faltered. "This is my brother!"

"Your *brother? - what? - eh?*" choked the Senior Surgeon. Bluntly he reached out and crushed the young fellow's fingers in his own. "Glad to see you, Son!" he muttered with a sickish sort of grin, and turning abruptly, picked up his baggage again and started for the big house.

Half a step behind him his White Linen Bride followed softly.

At the edge of the piazza he turned for an instant and eyed her a bit quizzically. With her big credulous blue eyes, and her great mop of yellow hair braided childishly down her back, she looked inestimably more juvenile and innocent than his own little shrewd-faced six-year-old whom he had just left domestically ensconced in the middle of the broad gravel path.

"For Heaven's sake, Miss Malgregor," he asked. "For Heaven's sake - why didn't you tell me that the Wall Paper Man was your - brother?"

Very contritely the White Linen Nurse's chin went burrowing down into the soft collar of her dress and as bashfully as a child one finger came stealing up to the edge of her red, red lips.

"I was afraid you'd think I was - cheeky - having any of my family come and live with us - so soon," she murmured almost inaudibly.

"Well, what did you think I'd think you were - if he wasn't your brother?" asked the Senior Surgeon sardonically.

"Very - economical, I hoped!" beamed the White Linen Nurse.

"All the same!" snapped the Senior Surgeon, with an

irrelevance surprising even to himself. "All the same do you think it sounds quite right and proper for a child to call her - step-mother - 'Peach'?"

Again the White Linen Nurse's chin went burrowing down into the soft collar of her dress. "I don't suppose it is - usual," she admitted reluctantly. "The children next door, I notice, call theirs - 'Cross-Patch.'"

With a gesture of impatience the Senior Surgeon proceeded up the steps, - yanked open the old-fashioned shuttered door, and burst quite breathlessly and unprepared upon his most amazingly reconstructed house. All in one single second chintzes, - muslins, - pale blonde maples, - riotous canary birds, - stormed revolutionary upon his outraged eyes. Reeling back utterly aghast before the sight, he stood there staring dumbly for an instant at what he considered, - and rightly too, - the absolute wreck of his black walnut home.

"It looks like - Hell!" he muttered feebly.

"Yes, *isn't* it sweet?" conceded the White Linen Nurse with unmistakable joyousness. "And your library -" Triumphantly she threw back the door to his grim work-shop.

"Good God!" stammered the Senior Surgeon. "You've made it - pink!"

Rapturously the White Linen Nurse began to clasp and unclasp her hands. "I knew you'd love it!" she said.

Half dazed with bewilderment the Senior Surgeon started to brush an imaginary haze from his eyes but paused mid-way in the gesture and pointed back instead to a dapper little hall-table that seemed to be exhausting its entire blonde strength in holding up a slender green vase with a single pink rose in it. Like a caged animal buffeting for escape against each successive bar that incased it, the man's frenzied irritation hurled itself hopefully against this one more chance for explosive exit.

"What - have - you - done - with the big - black - escritoire that stood - there?" he demanded accusingly.

"Escritoire? - Escritoire?" worried the White Linen Nurse. "Why - why - I'm afraid I must have mislaid it."

"Mislaid it?" thundered the Senior Surgeon. "Mislaid it? It weighed three hundred pounds!"

"Oh, it did?" questioned the White Linen Nurse with great, blue-eyed interest. Still mulling apparently over the fascinating weight of the escritoire she climbed up suddenly into a chair and with the fluffy broom-shaped end of her extraordinarily long braid of hair went angling wildy off into space after an illusive cobweb.

Faster and faster the Senior Surgeon's temper began to search for a new point of exit.

"What do you suppose the - servants think of you?" he stormed. "Running round like that with your hair in a pig-tail like a - kid?"

"Servants?" cooed the White Linen Nurse. "Servants?" Very quietly she jumped down from the chair and came and stood looking up into the Senior Surgeon's hectic face. "Why, there aren't any servants," she explained patiently. "I've dismissed every one of them. We're doing our own work now!"

"Doing 'our own work'?" gasped the Senior Surgeon.

Quite worriedly the White Linen Nurse stepped back a little. "Why, wasn't that right?" she pleaded. "Wasn't it right? Why, I thought people always did their own work when they were first married!" With sudden apprehensiveness she glanced round over her shoulder at the hall clock, and darting out through a side door, returned almost instantly with a fierce-looking knife.

"I'm so late now and everything," she confided. "Could you peel the potatoes for me?"

"No, I couldn't!" said the Senior Surgeon shortly. Equally shortly he turned on his heel, and reaching out once more for his rod-case and grip went on up the stairs to his own room.

One of the pleasantest things about arriving home very late in the afternoon is the excuse it gives you for loafing in your own room while other people are getting supper. No existent domestic sound in the whole twenty-four hours is as soothing at the end of a long journey as the sound of other people getting supper.

Stretched out full length in a big easy chair by his bed-room window, with his favorite pipe bubbling rhythmically between his gleaming white teeth, the Senior Surgeon studied his new "solid gold bed" and his new sage green wall-paper and his new dust-colored rug, to the faint, far-away accompaniment of soft thudding feet, and a girl's laugh, and a child's prattle, and the tink-tink-tinkle of glass, - china, - silver, - all scurrying consciously to the service of one man, - and that man, - *himself*.

Very, very slowly, in that special half hour an inscrutable little smile printed itself experimentally across the right hand corner of the Senior Surgeon's upper lip.

While that smile was still in its infancy he jumped up suddenly and forced his way across the hall to his dead wife's room, - the one ghost-room of his house and his life, - and there with his hand on the turning door knob, - tense with reluctance, - goose-fleshed with strain, - his breath gasped out of him whether or no with the one word - "Alice!"

And behold! There was no room there!

Lurching back from the threshold, as from the brink of an elevator well, the Senior Surgeon found himself staring foolishly into a most sumptuous linen closet, tiered like an Aztec cliff with home after home for pleasant prosy blankets, and gaily fringed towels, and cheerful white sheets reeking most conscientiously of cedar and lavender. Tiptoeing cautiously into the mystery he sensed at one astonished, grateful glance how the change of a partition, the re-adjustment of a proportion, had purged like a draft of fresh air the stale gloom of an ill-favored memory. Yet so inevitable did it suddenly seem for a linen closet to be built right there, - so inevitable did it suddenly seem for the child's meager play-room to be enlarged just there, that to save his soul he could not estimate whether the happy plan had originated in a purely practical brain or a purely compassionate heart.

Half proud of the brain, half touched by the heart, he passed on exploringly through the new play-room out into the hall again.

Quite distinctly now through the aperture of the back stairs the kitchen voices came wafting up to him.

"Oh, dear! Oh, dear!" wailed his Little Girl's peevish voice. "Now that - that Man's come back again - I suppose we'll have to eat in the dining-room - all the time!"

"'That Man' happens to be your darling father!" admonished the White Linen Nurse's laughing voice.

"Even so," wailed the Little Girl, "I love you best."

"Even so," laughed the White Linen Nurse, "I love *you* best!"

"Just the same," cried the Little Girl shrilly, "just the same - let's put the cream pitcher way up high somewhere - so he can't step in it!"

As though from a head tilted suddenly backward the White Linen Nurse's laugh rang out in joyous abandon.

Impulsively the Senior Surgeon started to grin. Then equally impulsively the grin soured on his lips. So they thought he was clumsy? Eh? Resentfully he stared down at his hands, - those wonderfully dexterous, - yes, ambidexterous hands that were the aching envy of all his colleagues. Interruptingly as he stared the voice of the young Wall Paper Man rose buoyantly from the lower hallway.

"Supper's all ready, sir!" called the cordial voice.

For some inexplainable reason, at that particular moment, almost nothing in the world could have irritated the Senior Surgeon more keenly than to be invited to his own supper, - in his own house, - by a stranger. Fuming with a new sense of injury and injustice he started heavily down the stairs to the dining-room.

Standing patiently behind the Senior Surgeon's chair with a laudable desire to assist his carving in any possible emergency that might occur, the White Linen Nurse experienced her first direct marital rebuff.

"What do you think this is? An autopsy?" demanded the Senior Surgeon tartly. "For Heaven's sake - sit down!"

Quite meekly the White Linen Nurse subsided into her place.

The meal that ensued could hardly have been called a success though the room was entrancing, - the cloth, snow-white - the silver, radiant, - the guinea chicken beyond reproach.

Swept and garnished to an alarming degree the young Wall Paper Man presided over the gravy and did his uttermost, innocent country-best to make the Senior Surgeon feel perfectly at home.

Conscientiously, as in the presence of a distinguished stranger, the Little Crippled Girl most palpably from time to time repressed her insatiable desire to build a towering pyramid out of all the salt and pepper shakers she could reach.

Once when the young Wall Paper Man forgot himself to the extent of putting his knife in his mouth, the White Linen Nurse jarred the whole table with the violence of her warning kick.

Once when the Little Crippled Girl piped out impulsively, "Say, Peach, - what was the name of that bantam your father used to fight against the minister's bantam?" the White Linen Nurse choked piteously over her food.

Twice some one spoke about this year's weather.

Twice some one volunteered an illuminating remark about last year's weather.

Except for these four diversions restraint indescribable hung like a horrid pall over the feast.

Next to feeling unwelcome in your friend's house, nothing certainly is more wretchedly disconcerting than to feel unwelcome in your own house!

Grimly the Senior Surgeon longed to grab up all the knives within reach and ram them successively into his own mouth just to prove to the young Wall Paper Man what a - what a devil of a good fellow he was himself! Grimly the Senior Surgeon longed to tell the White Linen Nurse about the pet bantam of his own boyhood days - that he bet a dollar could lick any bantam her father ever dreamed of owning! Grimly the Senior Surgeon longed to talk dolls, - dishes, - kittens, - yes, even cream pitchers, to his Little Daughter, to talk anything in fact - to *any one*, - to talk - sing - shout *anything* - that should make him, at least for the time being, one at heart, one at head, one at table, with this astonishingly offish bunch of youngsters!

But grimly instead, - out of his frazzled nerves, - out of his innate spiritual bashfulness, he merely roared forth, "Where are the potatoes?"

"Potatoes?" gasped the White Linen Nurse. "Potatoes? Oh, potatoes?" she finished more blithely. "Why, yes, of course! Don't you remember - you didn't have time to peel them for me? I was so disappointed!"

"You were so disappointed?" snapped the Senior Surgeon. "You? - you?"

Janglingly the Little Crippled Girl knelt right up in her chair and shook her tiny fist right in her father's face.

"Now, Lendicott Paber!" she screamed. "Don't you start in - sassing - my darling little Peach!"

"*Peach?*" snorted the Senior Surgeon. With almost supernatural calm he put down his knife and fork and eyed his offspring with an expression of absolutely inflexible purpose. "Don't you - ever," he warned her, "ever - ever - let me hear you call - this woman 'Peach' again!"

A trifle faint-heartedly the Little Crippled Girl reached up and straightened her absurdly diminutive little white cap, and pursed her little mouth as nearly as possible into an expression of ineffable peace.

"Why - Lendicott Faber!" she persisted heroically.

"*Lendicott?*" jumped the Senior Surgeon. "What are *you* - 'Lendicotting' *me* for?"

Hilariously with her own knife and fork the Little Crippled Girl began to beat upon the table.

"Why, you dear Silly!" she cried. "Why, if I'm the new Marma, I've got to call you 'Lendicott'! And Peach has got to call you 'Fat Father'!"

Frenziedly the Senior Surgeon pushed back his chair, and jumped to his feet. The expression on his face was neither smile nor frown, nor war nor peace, nor any other human expression that had ever puckered there before.

"God!" he said. "This gives me the *willies*!" and strode tempestuously from the room.

Out in his own work-shop fortunately, - whatever the grotesque new pinkness, - whatever the grotesque new perkiness - his great free walking-spaces had not been interfered with. Slamming his door triumphantly behind him, he resumed once more the monotonous pace-pace-pace that had characterized for eighteen years his first night's return to - the obligations of civilization.

Sharply around the corner of his old battered desk the little path started, - wanly along the edge of his dingy book-shelves the little path furrowed, - wistfully at the deep bay-window where his favorite lilac bush budded whitely for his departure, and rusted brownly for his return, the little path faltered, - and went on again, - on and on and on, - into the alcove where his instruments glistened, - up to the fireplace where his college trophy-cups tarnished! Listlessly the Senior Surgeon recommenced his yearly vigil. Up and down, - up and down, - round and round, - on and on and on, - through interminable dusks to unattainable dawns, - a glutted, bacchanalian Soul sweating its own way back to sanctity and leanness! Nerves always were in that vigil, - raw, rattling nerves clamoring vociferously to be repacked in their sedatives. Thirst also was in that vigil, - no mere whimpering tickle of the palate, but a drought of the tissues, - a consuming fire of the bones! Hurt pride was also there, and festering humiliation!

But more rasping, this particular night, than nerves, more poignant than thirst, more dangerously excitative even than remorse, hunger rioted in him, - hunger, the one worst enemy of the Senior Surgeon's cause, - the simple, silly, no-account, - gnawing, - drink-provocative hunger of an empty stomach.

And 'one other hunger was also there, - a sudden fierce new lust for Life and Living, - a passion bare of love yet pure of wantonness, - a passion primitive, - protective, - inexorably proprietary, - engendered strangely in that one mad, suspicious moment at the edge of the summer house when every outraged male instinct in him had leaped to prove that - love or no love - the woman was - *his*. Up and down, - up and down, - round and round, - eight o'clock found the Senior Surgeon still pacing.

At half past eight the young Wall Paper Man came to say good-by to him.

"As long as Sister won't be alone any more, I guess I'll be moving on," beamed the Wall Paper Man. "There's a dance at home Saturday night. And I've got a girl of my own!" he confided genially.

"Come again," urged the Senior Surgeon. "Come again when you can stay longer!"

With one honest prayer in stock, and at least two purely automatic social speeches of this sort, no man needs to flounder altogether hopelessly for words in any ordinary emergency of life. Thus with no more mental interruption than the two-minute break in time, the Senior Surgeon then resumed his bitter-thoughted pacing.

At nine o'clock, however, - patroling his long rangy book-shelves, he sensed with a very different feeling through his heavy oak door, the soft whirring swish of skirts and the breathy twitter of muffled voices. Faintly to his acute ears came the sound of his little daughter's temperish protest, "I won't! I won't!" and the White Linen Nurse's fervid pleading, "Oh, you must, - you must!" and the Little Girl's mumbled ultimatum, "Well, I won't unless *you* do!"

Irascibly he crossed the room and yanked the door open abruptly upon their surprise and confusion. His nerves were very sore.

"What in thunder do you want?" he snarled.

Nervously for an instant the White Linen Nurse tugged at the Little Girl's hand. Nervously for an instant the Little Girl tugged at the White Linen Nurse's hand. Then with a swallow like a sob the White Linen Nurse lifted her glowing face to his.

"K - kiss us good night!" said the White Linen Nurse.

Telescopically all in that startling second, vision after vision beat down like blows upon the Senior Surgeon's senses! The pink, pink flush of the girl! The lure of her! The amazing sweetness! The physical docility! Oh ye gods, - the docility! Every trend of her birth, - of her youth, - of her training, - forcing her now - if he chose it - to unquestioning submission to his will and his judgment! Faster and faster the temptation surged through his pulses! The path from her lips to her ear was such a little path, - the plea so quick to make, so short, - "I want you *now!*"

"K - kiss us good night!" urged the Big Girl's unsuspecting lips. "Kiss us good night!" mocked the Little Girl's tremulous echo.

Then explosively with the noblest rudeness of his life, "No, I *won't!*" said the Senior Surgeon, and slammed the door in their faces.

Falteringly up the stairs he heard the two ascending, - speechless with surprise, perhaps, - stunned by his roughness, - still hand in hand, probably, - still climbing slowly bed-ward, - the soft, smooth, patient footfall of the White Linen Nurse and the jerky, laborious clang-clang-clang of a little dragging iron-braced leg.

Up and down, - round and round, - on and on and on, - the Senior Surgeon resumed his pacing. Under his eyes great shadows darkened. Along the corners of his mouth the lines furrowed like gray scars. Up and down, - round and round, - on and on and on - and on!

At ten o'clock, sitting bolt upright in her bed with her worried eyes straining bluely out across the Little Girl's somnolent form into unfathomable darkness, the White Linen Nurse in the throb of her own heart began to keep pace with that faint, horrid thud-thud-thud in the room below. Was he passing the book-case now? Had he reached the bay-window? Was he dawdling over those glistening scalpels? Would his nerves remember the flask in that upper desk drawer? Up and down, - round and round, - on and on, - the harrowing sound continued.

Resolutely at last she scrambled out of her snug nest, and hurrying into her great warm, pussy-gray wrapper began at once very practically, very unemotionally, with matches and alcohol and a shiny glass jar to prepare a huge steaming cup of malted milk. Beef-steak was infinitely better, she knew, or eggs, of course, but if she should venture forth to the kitchen for real substantiate the Senior Surgeon, she felt quite positive, would almost certainly hear her and stop her. So very stealthily thus like the proverbial assassin she crept down the front stairs with the innocent malted milk cup in her hand, and then with her knuckles just on the verge of rapping against the grimly inhospitable door, went suddenly paralyzed with uncertainty whether to advance or retreat.

Once again through the sombre inert wainscoting, exactly as if a soul had creaked, the Senior Surgeon sensed the threatening, intrusive presence of an unseen personality. Once again he strode across the room and jerked the door open with terrifying anger and resentment.

As though frozen there on his threshold by Her own little bare feet, - as though strangled there in his doorway by her own great mop of golden hair, - stolid and dumb as a pink-cheeked graven image the White Linen Nurse thrust the cup out awkwardly at him.

Absolutely without comment, as though she trotted on purely professional business and the case involved was of mutual concern to them both, the Senior Surgeon took the cup from her hand and closed the door again in her face.

At eleven o'clock she came again, - just as pink, - just as blue, - just as gray, - just as golden. And the cup of malted milk she brought with her was just as huge, - just as hot, - just as steaming, - only this time she had smuggled two raw eggs into it.

Once more the Senior Surgeon took the cup without comment and shut the door in her face.

At twelve o'clock she came again. The Senior Surgeon was unusually loquacious this time.

"Have you any more malted milk?" he asked tersely.

"Oh, yes, sir!" beamed the White Linen Nurse.

"Go and get it!" said the Senior Surgeon.

Obediently the White Linen Nurse pattered up the stairs and returned with the half depleted bottle. Frankly interested she recrossed the threshold of the room and delivered her glass treasure into the hands of the Senior Surgeon as he stood by his desk. Raising herself to her tiptoes she noted with eminent satisfaction that the three big cups on the other side of the desk had all been drained to their dregs.

Then very bluntly before her eyes the Senior Surgeon took the malted milk bottle and poured its remaining contents out quite wantonly into his waste basket. Then equally bluntly he took the White Linen Nurse by the shoulders and marched her out of the room.

"For God's sake!" he said, "get out of this room! And stay out!"

Bang! the big door slammed behind her. Like a snarling fang the lock bit into its catch.

"Yes, sir," said the White Linen Nurse. Even just to herself - all alone there in the big black hall, she was perfectly polite. "Y-e-s, sir," she repeated softly.

With a slightly sardonic grin on his face the Senior Surgeon resumed his pacing. Up and down, - round and round, - on and on and on!

At one o'clock in the dull, clammy chill of earliest morning he stopped long enough to light his hearthfire.

At two o'clock he stopped again to pile on a trifle more wood.

At three o'clock he dallied for an instant to close a window. The new day seemed strangely cold.

At four o'clock, dawn the wonder, - the miracle, - the long despaired of, - quickened wanly across the East. Then suddenly, - more like a phosphorescent breeze than a glow, the pale, pale yellow sunshine came wafting through the green gloom of the garden. The vigil was over!

Stumbling out into the shadowy hall to greet the new day and the new beginning, the Senior Surgeon almost tripped and fell over the White Linen Nurse sitting all huddled up and drowsy-eyed in a little gray heap on his outer threshold. The sensation of stepping upon a human body is not a pleasant one. It smote the Senior Surgeon nauseously through the nerves of his stomach.

"What are you doing here?" he fairly screamed at her.

"Just keeping you company, sir," yawned the White Linen Nurse. Before her hand could reach her mouth again another great childish yawn overwhelmed her. "Just - watching with you, sir," she finished more or less inarticulately.

"Watching with - me?" snarled the Senior Surgeon resentfully. "Why - should - you - watch - with - me?"

Like the frightened flash of a bird the heavy lashes went swooping down across the pink cheeks and lifted as suddenly again. "Because you're my - *man!*" yawned the White Linen Nurse.

Almost roughly the Senior Surgeon reached down and pulled the White Linen Nurse to her feet.

"God!" said the Senior Surgeon. In his strained, husky voice the word sounded like an oath. Grotesquely a little smile went scudding zig-zag across his haggard face. With an impulse absolutely alien to him he reached out abruptly again and raised the White Linen Nurse's hand to his lips. "'*Good* God' was what I meant - Miss Malgregor!" he grinned a bit sheepishly.

Quite bruskly then he turned and looked at his watch.

"I'd like my breakfast just as soon now as you can possibly get it!" heordered peremptorily, - in his own morbid pathological emergency no more stopping to consider the White Linen Nurse's purely normal fatigue, than he in any pathological emergency of hers would have stopped to consider his own comfort, - safety, - or even perhaps, life!

Joyously then like a prisoner just turned loose, he went swinging up the stairs to recreate himself with a smoke and a shave and a great, splashing, cold shower-bath.

Only one thing seemed to really trouble him now. At the top of the stairs he stopped for an instant and cocked his head a bit worriedly towards the drawing-room where from some slow-brightening alcove bird-carol after bird-carol went fluting shrilly up into the morning.

"Is that - those blasted canaries?" he asked briefly.

Very companionably the White Linen Nurse cocked her own towsled head on one side and listened with him for half a moment.

"Only four of them are blasted canaries," she corrected very gently. "The fifth one is a paroquet that I got at a mark-down because it was a widowed bird and wouldn't mate again."

"Eh?" jerked the Senior Surgeon.

"Yes, sir," said the White Linen Nurse and started for the kitchen.

No one but the Senior Surgeon himself breakfasted in state at five o'clock that morning. Snug and safe in her crib upstairs the Little Crippled Girl slumbered peacefully on through the general disturbance. And as for the White Linen Nurse herself, - what with chilling and rechilling melons, - and broiling and unbroiling steaks, - and making and remaking coffee, - and hunting frantically for a different-sized water glass, - or a prettier colored plate, there was no time for anything except an occasional hurried surreptitious nibble half way between the stove and the table.

Yet in all that raucous early morning hour together neither man nor girl suffered towards the other the slightest personal sense of contrition or resentment, for each mind was trained equally fairly, - whether reacting on its own case or another's - to differentiate pretty readily between mean nerves and a - mean spirit.

Only once in fact across the intervening chasm of crankiness did the Senior Surgeon hurl a smile that was even remotely self-conscious or conciliatory. Glancing up suddenly from a particularly sharp and disagreeable speech, he noted the White

Linen Nurse's red lips mumbling softly one to the other.

"Are you specially - religious, - Miss Malgregor?" he grinned quite abruptly.

"No, not specially, sir," said the White Linen Nurse. "Why, sir?"

"Oh, it 's only -" grinned the Senior Surgeon dourly, "it's only that every time I'm especially ugly to you, I see your lips moving as though in 'silent prayer' as they call it - and I was just wondering - if there was any special formula you used with me - that kept you so - everlastingly - damned serene. Is there?"

"Yes, sir," said the White Linen Nurse.

"What is it?" demanded the Senior Surgeon quite bluntly.

"Do I have to tell?" gasped the White Linen Nurse. A little tremulously in her hand the empty cup she was carrying rattled against its saucer. "Do I have to tell?" she repeated pleadingly.

A delirious little thrill of power went fluttering through the Senior Surgeon's heart.

"Yes, you have to tell me!" he announced quite seriously.

In absolute submission to his demand, though with very palpable reluctance, the White Linen Nurse came forward to the table, put down the cup and saucer, and began to finger a trifle nervously at the cloth.

"Oh, I'm sure I didn't mean any harm, sir," she stammered. "But all I say is, - honest and truly all I say is, - 'Bah! He's nothing but a man - nothing but a man - nothing but a man!' over and over and over, - just that, sir!"

Uproariously the Senior Surgeon pushed back his chair, and

jumped to his feet.

"I guess after all I'll have to let the little kid call you - 'Peach' - one day a week!" he acknowledged jocosely.

With infinite seriousness then he tossed back his great splendid head, - shook himself free apparently from all unhappy memories, - and started for his work-room, - a great gorgeously vital, extraordinarily talented, gray-haired *boy* lusting joyously for his own work and play again - after a month's distressing illness!

From the edge of the hall he turned round and made a really boyish grimace at her.

"Now if I only had the horns or the cloven hoof - that you think I have," he called, "what an easy time I'd make of it, raking over all the letters and ads. that are stacked up on my desk!"

"Yes, sir," said the White Linen Nurse.

Only once did he come back into the kitchen or dining-room for anything. It was at seven o'clock. And the White Linen Nurse was still washing dishes.

As radiant as a gray-haired god he towered up in the doorway. The boyish rejuvenation in him was even more startling than before.

"I'm feeling so much like a fighting cock this morning," he said, "I think I'll tackle that paper on surgical diseases of the pancreas that I have to read at Baltimore next month!" A little startlingly the gray lines furrowed into his cheeks again. "For Heaven's sake - see that I'm not disturbed by anything!" he admonished her warningly.

It must have been almost eight o'clock when the ear-splitting scream from upstairs sent the White Linen Nurse plunging out panic-stricken into the hall.

"Oh, Peach! Peach!" yelled the Little Girl's frenzied voice. "Come quick and see - what Fat Father's doing *now* - out on the piazza!"

Jerkily the White Linen Nurse swerved off through the French door that opened directly on the piazza. Had the Senior Surgeon hung himself, she tortured, in some wild, temporary aberration of the "morning after"?

But staunchly and reassuringly from the further end of the *piazza* the Senior Surgeon's broad back belied her horrid terror. Quite prosily and in apparently perfect health he was standing close to the railing of the piazza. On a table directly beside him rested four empty bird cages. Just at that particular moment he was inordinately busy releasing the last canary from the fifth cage. Both hands were smouched with ink and behind his left ear a fountain pen dallied daringly.

At the very first sound of the White Linen Nurse's step the Senior Surgeon turned and faced her with a sheepish sort of defiance.

"Well, now, I imagine," he said, "well, now, I imagine I've really made you - mad!"

"No, not mad, sir," faltered the White Linen Nurse. "No, not mad, sir, - but very far from well." Coaxingly with a perfectly futile hand she tried to lure one astonished yellow songster back from a swaying yellow bush. "Why, they'll die, sir!" she protested. "Savage cats will get them!"

"It's a choice of their lives - or mine!" said the Senior Surgeon tersely.

"Yes, sir," droned the White Linen Nurse.

Quite snappishly the Senior Surgeon turned upon her. "For

Heaven's sake - do you think - canary birds are more valuable than I am?" he demanded stentoriously.

Most disconcertingly before his glowering eyes a great, sad, round tear rolled suddenly down the White Linen Nurse's flushed cheek.

"N - o, - not more valuable," conceded the White Linen Nurse. "But more - c-cunning."

Up to the roots of the Senior Surgeon's hair a flush of real contrition spread hotly.

"Why - Rae!" he stammered. "Why, what a beast I am! Why - ! Why!" In sincere perplexity he began to rack his brains for some adequate excuse, - some adequate explanation. "Why, I'm sure I didn't mean to make you feel badly," he persisted. "Only I've lived alone so long that I suppose I've just naturally drifted into the way of having a thing if I wanted it and - throwing it away if I didn't! And canary birds, now? Well - really -" he began to glower all over again. "Oh, thunder!" he finished abruptly, "I guess I'll go on down to the hospital where I belong!"

A little wistfully the White Linen Nurse stepped forward. "The hospital?" she said. "Oh, - the hospital? Do you think that perhaps you could come home a little bit earlier than usual - to-night - and - and help me catch - just one of the canaries?"

"What?" gasped the Senior Surgeon. Incredulously with a very inky finger he pointed at his own breast. "What? I?" he demanded. "I? Come home - early - from the hospital to help - you - catch a canary?"

Disgustedly without further comment he turned and stalked back again into the house.

The disgust was still in his walk as he left the house an hour later. Watching his exit down the long gravel path the Little

Crippled Girl commented audibly on the matter.

"Peach! Peach!" called the Little Crippled Girl. "What makes Fat Father walk so - surprised?"

People at the hospital also commented upon him.

"Gee!" giggled the new nurses. "We bet he 's a Tartar! But isn't his hair cute? And say -" gossiped the new nurses, "is it really true that that Malgregor girl was pinned down perfectly helpless under the car and he wouldn't let her out till she'd promised to marry him? Isn't it *awful?* Isn't it *romantic*?"

"Why! Dr. Faber 's back!" fluttered the senior nurses. "Isn't he wonderful? Isn't he beautiful? But, oh, say," they worried, "what do you suppose Rae ever finds to talk with him about? Would she ever dare talk *things* to him, - just plain every-day *things*, - hats, and going to the theater, and what to have for breakfast? - breakfast?" they gasped. "Why, yes, of course!" they reasoned more sanely. "Steak? Eggs? Even oatmeal? Why, people had to eat - no matter how wonderful they were! But evenings?" they speculated more darkly. "But evenings?" In the whole range of human experience - was it even so much as remotely imaginable that - evenings - the Senior Surgeon and - Rae Malgregor - sat in the hammock and held hands? "Oh, Gee!" blanched the senior nurses.

"Good-morning, Dr. Faber!" greeted the Superintendent of Nurses from behind her austere office desk.

"Good-morning, Miss Hartzen!" said the Senior Surgeon.

"Have you had a pleasant trip?" quizzed the Superintendent of Nurses.

"Exceptionally so, thank you!" said the Senior Surgeon.

"And - Mrs. Faber, - is she well?" persisted the Superintendent of Nurses conscientiously.

"Mrs. Faber?" gasped the Senior Surgeon. "Mrs. Faber? Oh, yes! Why, of course! Yes, indeed - she's extraordinarily well! I never saw her better!"

"She must have been - very lonely without you - this past month?" rasped the Superintendent of Nurses - perfectly politely.

"Yes - she was," flushed the Senior Surgeon. "She - she suffered - keenly!"

"And you, too?" drawled the Superintendent of Nurses. "It must have been very hard for you."

"Yes, it was!" sweated the Senior Surgeon. "I suffered keenly, too!"

Distractedly he glanced back at the open door. An extraordinarily large number of nurses, internes, orderlies, seemed to be having errands up and down the corridor that allowed them a peculiarly generous length of neck to stretch into the Superintendent's office.

"Great Heavens!" snapped the Senior Surgeon. "What 's the matter with everybody this morning?" Tempestuously he started for the door. "Hurry up my cases, please, Miss Hartzen!" he ordered. "Send them to the operating room! And let me get to work!"

At eleven o'clock, absolutely calm, absolutely cool, - pure as a girl in his fresh, white operating clothes - cleaner, - skin, hair, teeth, hands, - than any girl who ever walked the face of the earth, in a white tiled room as surgically clean as himself, with three or four small, glistening instruments still boiling, steaming hot - and half a dozen breathless assistants almost as immaculate as himself, with his gown, cap and mask adjusted, his gloves finally on, and the faintest possible little grin twitching oddly at the corner of his mouth, he "went in" as they say, to a new born baby's tortured, twisted spine - and took out - fifty years perhaps of hunched-back pain and shame and morbid passions flourishing banefully in the dark shades of a disordered life.

At half-past twelve he did an appendix operation on the only son of his best friend. At one o'clock he did another appendix operation. Whom it was on didn't matter. It couldn't have been worse on - any one. At half-past one no one remembered to feed him. At two, in another man's operation, he saw the richest merchant in the city go wafted out into eternity on the fumes of ether taken for the lancing of a stye. At three o'clock, passing the open door of one of the public waiting-rooms, an Italian peasant woman rushed out and spat in his face because her tubercular daughter had just died at the sanitarium where the Senior Surgeon's money had sent her. Only in this one wild, defiling moment did the lust for alcohol surge up in him again, surge clamorously, brutally, absolutely mercilessly, as though in all the known cleansants of the world only interminable raw whisky was hot enough to cauterize a polluted consciousness. At half past three, as soon as he could change his clothes again, he re-broke and re-set an acrobat's priceless leg. At five o'clock, more to rest himself than anything else, he went up to the autopsy amphitheater to look over an exhibit of enlarged hearts, whose troubles were permanently over.

At six o'clock just as he was leaving the great building with all its harrowing sights, sounds, and smells, a peremptory telephone call from one of the younger surgeons of the city summoned him back into the stuffy office again.

"Dr. Faber?"

"Yes."

"This is Merkley!"

"Yes."

"Can you come immediately and help me with that fractured skull case I was telling you about this morning? We'll have to trepan right away!"

"Trepan nothing!" grunted the Senior Surgeon. "I've got to go home early to-night - and help catch a canary."

"Catch a - what?" gasped the younger surgeon.

"A canary!" grinned the Senior Surgeon mirthlessly.

"A - *what?*" roared the younger man.

"Oh, shut up, you damned fool! Of course I'll come!" said the Senior Surgeon.

There was no "boy" left in the Senior Surgeon when he reached home that night.

Gray with road-travel, haggard with strain and fatigue, it was long, long after the rosy sunset time, - long, long after the yellow supper light, that he came dragging up through the sweet-scented dusk of the garden and threw himself down without greeting of any sort on the top step of the piazza where the White Linen Nurse's skirts glowed palely through the gloom.

"Well, I put a canary bird back into its cage for you!" he confided laconically. "It was a little chap's soul. It sure would have gotten away before morning."

"Who was the man that tried to turn it loose - *this* time?" asked the White Linen Nurse.

"I didn't say that anybody did!" growled the Senior Surgeon.

"Oh," said the White Linen Nurse. "Oh." Quite palpably a little shiver of flesh and starch went rustling through her. "I've had a wonderful day, too!" she confided softly. "I've cleaned the attic and darned nine pairs of your stockings and bought a sewing-machine - and started to make you a white silk negligee shirt for a surprise!"

"Eh?" jerked the Senior Surgeon.

The jerk seemed to liberate suddenly the faint vibration of dishes and the sound of ice knocking lusciously against a glass.

"Oh, have you had any supper, sir?" asked the White Linen Nurse.

With a prodigious sigh the Senior Surgeon threw his head back against the piazza railing and stretched his legs a little further out along the piazza floor.

"Supper?" he groaned. "No! Nor dinner! Nor breakfast! Nor any other - blankety-blank meal as far back as I can remember!" Janglingly in his voice, fatigue, hunger, nerves, crashed together like the slammed notes of a piano. "But I wouldn't - move - now," he snarled, "if all the blankety-blank-blank foods in Christendom - were piled blankety-blank-blank high - on all the blankety-blank-blank tables - in this whole blankety-blank-blank house!"

Ecstatically the White Linen Nurse clapped her hands. "Oh, that's just exactly what I hoped you'd say!" she cried. "'Cause the supper's - right here!"

"Here?" snapped the Senior Surgeon. Tempestuously he began all over again. "I - tell - you - I - wouldn't - lift - my - little finger - if all the blankety-blank-blank-blank -"

"Oh, Goody then!" said the White Linen Nurse. "'Cause now I can feed you! I sort of miss fussing with the canary birds," she added wistfully.

"Feed me?" roared the Senior Surgeon. Again something started a lump of ice tinkling faintly in a thin glass. "Feed me?"

he began all over again.

Yet with a fragrant strawberry half as big as a peach held out suddenly under his nose, just from sheer, irresistible instinct he bit out at it - and nipped the White Linen Nurse's finger instead.

"Ouch - sir!" said the White Linen Nurse.

Mumblingly down from an upstairs window, as from a face flatted smouchingly against a wire screen, a peremptory summons issued.

"Peach! - Peach!" called an angry little voice. "If you don't come to bed - now - I'll - I'll say my curses instead of my prayers!"

A trifle nervously the White Linen Nurse scrambled to her feet.

"Maybe I'd - better go?" she said.

"Maybe - you had!" said the Senior Surgeon quite definitely.

At the edge of the threshold the White Linen Nurse turned for an instant.

"Good-night, Dr. Faber!" she whispered.

"Good-night, Rae Malgregor - Faber!" said the Senior Surgeon.

"Good-night - *what?*" gasped the White Linen Nurse.

"Good-night, Rae Malgregor - Faber," repeated the Senior Surgeon.

Clutching at her skirts as though a mouse were after her, the White Linen Nurse went scuttling up the stairs.

Very late - on into the night - the Senior Surgeon lay there on his piazza floor staring out into his garden. Very companionably from time to time, like a tame firefly, a little bright spark hovered and glowed for an instant above the bowl of his pipe. Puff-puff-puff, doze-doze-doze, throb-throb-throb, - on and on and on and on - into the sweet-scented night.

CHAPTER X

So the days passed. And the nights. And more days. And more nights. July - August, - on and on and on.

Strenuous, nerve-racking, heart-breaking surgical days - broken maritally only by the pleasant, soft-worded greeting at the gate, or the practical, homely appeal of good food cooked with heart as well as hands, or the tingling, inciting masculine consciousness of there being a woman's - blush in the house!

Strenuous, house-working, child-nursing, home-making, domestic days - broken maritally only by the jaded, harsh word at the gate, the explosive criticism of food, the deadening, depressing, feminine consciousness of there being a man's - vicious temper in the house!

Now and again in one big automobile or another the White Linen Nurse and the Senior Surgeon rode out together, always and forever with the Little Crippled Girl sitting between them, - the other woman's little crippled girl. Now and again in the late summer afternoons the White Linen Nurse and the Senior Surgeon strolled together through the rainbow-colored garden, always and forever with the Little Crippled Girl, - the other woman's little crippled girl, tagging close behind them with her little sad, clanking leg. Now and again in the long sweet summer evenings the White Linen Nurse and the Senior Surgeon sat on the clematis-shadowed porch together, always and forever with the Little Crippled Girl, - the other woman's little crippled girl, mocking them querulously from some vague upper window.

Now and again across the mutually ghost-haunted chasm that separated them flashed the incontrovertible signal of sex and sense, as once when a new Interne, grossly bungling, stepped to the hospital window with a colleague to watch the Senior Surgeon's car roll away as usual with its two feminine passengers.

"What makes the Chief so stingy with that big handsome girl of his?" queried the new Interne a bit resentfully. "He won't ever bring her into the hospital! - won't ever ask any of us young chaps out to his house! And some of us come mighty near to being eligible, too! - Who's he saving her for, anyway? - A saint? - A miracle-worker? - A millionaire medicine man? - They don't exist, you know!"

"I'm saving her for myself!" snapped the Senior Surgeon most disconcertingly from the doorway. "She - she happens to be my wife, not my daughter, - thank you!"

When the Senior Surgeon went home that night he carried a big bunch of magazines and a box of candy as large as his head tucked courtingly under his arm.

Now and again across the chasm that separated them flashed the incontrovertible signal of mutual trust and appreciation, as when once, after a particularly violent vocal outburst on the Senior Surgeon's part, he sobered down very suddenly and said:

"Rae Malgregor, - do you realize that in all the weeks we've been together you've never once nagged me about my swearing? Not a word, - not a single word!"

"I'm not very used to - words," smiled the White Linen Nurse hopefully. "All I know how to nag with is - is raw eggs! If we could only get those nerves of yours padded just once, sir! The swearing would get well of itself."

In August the Senior Surgeon suggested sincerely that the house was much too big for the White Linen Nurse to run all alone, but conceded equally sincerely, under the White Linen Nurse's vehement protest, that servants, particularly new servants did creak considerably round a house, and that maybe "just for the present" at least, until he finished his very nervous paper on brain tumors perhaps it would be better to stay "just by ourselves."

In September the White Linen Nurse wanted very much to go home to Nova Scotia to her sister's wedding but the Senior Surgeon was trying a very complicated and worrisome new brace on the Little Girl's leg and it didn't seem quite kind to go. In October she planned her trip all over again. She was going to take the Little Crippled Girl with her this time. But with their trunks already packed and waiting in the hall, the Senior Surgeon came home from the hospital with a septic finger - and it didn't seem quite best to leave him.

"Well, how do you like being married *now?*" asked the Senior Surgeon a bit ironically in his work-room that night, after the White Linen Nurse had stood for an hour with evil-smelling washes, and interminable bandages trying to fix that finger the precise, particular way that he thought it ought to be fixed. "Well - how do you like - being married *now?*" he insisted trenchantly.

"Oh, I like it all right, sir!" said the White Linen Nurse. A little bit wanly this time she smiled her pluck up into the Senior Surgeon's questioning face. "Oh, I like it all right, sir! Oh, of course, sir," she confided thoughtfully - "Oh, of course, sir - it isn't quite as fancy as being engaged - or quite as free and easy as being - single. But still -" she admitted with desperate honesty - "but still there's a sort of - a sort of a combination importance and - and comfort about it, sir, like a - like a velvet suit - the second year, sir."

"Is that - all?" quizzed the Senior Surgeon bluntly.

"That's all - so far, sir," said the White Linen Nurse.

In November the White Linen Nurse caught a bit of cold that pulled her down a little. But the Senior Surgeon didn't notice it specially among all the virulent ills he lived and worked with from day to day. And then when the cold disappeared, Indian Summer came like a reeking sweat after a chill! And the house *was* big! And the Little Crippled Girl *was* pretty difficult to manage now and then! And the Senior Surgeon, no matter how hard he tried not to, did succeed somehow in creating more or less of a disturbance - at least every other day or two!

And then suddenly, one balmy gold and crimson Indian Summer morning, standing out on the piazza trying to hear what the Little Crippled Girl was calling from the window and what the Senior Surgeon was calling from the gate, the White Linen Nurse fell right down in her tracks, brutally, bulkily, like a worn-out horse, and lay as she fell, a huddled white heap across the gray piazza.

"Oh, Father! Come quick! Come quick! Peach has deaded herself!" yelledthe Little Girl's frantic voice.

Just with his foot on the step of his car the Senior Surgeon heard the cry and came speeding back up the long walk. Already there before him the Little Girl knelt raining passionate, agonized kisses on her beloved playmate's ghastly white face.

"Leave her alone!" thundered the Senior Surgeon. "Leave her alone, I say!"

Bruskly he pushed the Little Girl aside and knelt to cradle his own ear against the White Linen Nurse's heart.

"Oh, it's all right," he growled, and gathered the White Linen Nurse right up in his arms - she was startlingly lighter than he had supposed - and carried her up the stairs and put her to bed like a child in the great sumptuous guest-room, in a great sumptuous nest of all the best linens and blankets, with the Little Crippled Girl superintending the task with many hysterical suggestions and sharp staccato interruptions. For once in his life the Senior Surgeon did not stop to quarrel with his daughter.

Rallying limply from her swoon the White Linen Nurse stared out with hazy perplexity at last from her dimpling white pillows to see the Senior Surgeon standing amazingly at the guest-room bureau with a glass and a medicine-dropper in his hand, and the Little Crippled Girl hanging apparently by her narrow peaked chin across the foot-board of the bed.

Gazing down worriedly at the lace-ruffled sleeve of her night-dress the White Linen Nurse made her first public speech to the - world at large.

"Who - put - me - to - bed?" whispered the White Linen Nurse.

Ecstatically the Little Crippled Girl began to pound her fists on the foot-board of the bed.

"Father did!" she cried in unmistakable triumph. "All the little hooks! All the little buttons! - *wasn't* it cunning?"

The Senior Surgeon would hardly have been human if he hadn't glanced back suddenly over his shoulder at the White Linen Nurse's precipitously changing color. Quite irrepressibly, as he saw the red, red blood come surging home again into her cheeks, a little short chuckling laug escaped him.

"I guess you'll live - now," he remarked dryly.

Then because a Senior Surgeon can't stay home on the mere impulse of the moment from a great rushing hospital, just because one member of his household happens to faint perfectly innocently in the morning, he hurried on to his work again. And saved a little boy, and lost a little girl, and mended a fractured thigh, and eased a gun-shot wound, and camedashing home at noon in one of his thousand-dollar hours to feel the White Linen Nurse's pulse and broil her a bit of tenderloin steak with his own thousand-dollar hands, - and then went dashing off again to do one major operation or another, telephoned home once or twice during the afternoon to make sure that everything was all right, and finding that the White Linen Nurse was comfortably up and about again, went sprinting off fifty miles somewhere on a meningitis consultation, and came dragging home at last, somewhere near midnight, to a big black house brightened only by a single light in the kitchen where the White Linen Nurse went tiptoeing softly from stove to pantry in deft preparation of an appetizing supper for him.

Quite roughly again without smile or appreciation the Senior Surgeon took her by the shoulders and turned her out of the kitchen, and started her up the stairs.

"Are you an - idiot?" he said. "Are you an - imbecile?" he came back and called up the stairs to her just as she was disappearing from the upper landing.

Then up and down, round and round, on and on and on, the Senior Surgeon began suddenly to pace again.

Only, for some unexplainable reason to the White Linen Nurse upstairs, his work-room didn't seem quite large enough for his pacing this night Along the broad piazza she heard his footsteps creak. Far, far into the morning, lying warm and snug in her own little bed, she heard his footsteps crackling through the wet-leafed garden paths.

Yet the Senior Surgeon didn't look an atom jaded or forlorn when he came down to breakfast the next morning. He had on a brand new gray suit that fitted his big, powerful shoulders to perfection, and the glad glow of his shower-bath was still reddening faintly in his cheeks as he swung around the corner of the table and dropped down into his place with an odd little grin on his lips directed intermittently towards the White Linen Nurse and the Little Crippled Girl who already waited him there at either end of the table.

"Oh, Father, isn't it lovely to have my darling - darling Peach all well again!" beamed the Little Crippled Girl with unusual friendliness.

"Speaking of your - 'darling Peach,'" said the Senior Surgeon quite abruptly. "Speaking of your 'darling Peach,' - I'm going to - take her away with me to-day - for a week or so."

"Eh?" jumped the Little Crippled Girl.

"What? What, sir?" stammered the White Linen Nurse.

Quite prosily the Senior Surgeon began to butter a piece of toast. But the little twinkle around his eyes belied in some way the utter prosiness of the act.

"For a little trip," he confided amiably. "A little holiday!"

A trifle excitedly the White Linen Nurse laid down her knife and fork and stared at him, blue-eyed and wondering as a child.

"A holiday?" she gasped. "To a - beach, you mean? Would there be a - a roller-coaster? I've never seen a roller-coaster!"

"Eh?" laughed the Senior Surgeon.

"Oh, I'm going, too! I'm going, too!" piped the Little Crippled Girl.

Most jerkily the Senior Surgeon pushed back his chair from the table and swallowed half a cup of coffee at one single gulp.

"Going *three*, you mean?" he glowered at his little daughter. "Going *three*?" His comment that ensued was distinctly rough as far as diction was concerned, but the facial expression of ineffable peace that accompanied it would have made almost any phrase sound like a benediction. "Not by a - damned sight!" beamed the Senior Surgeon. "This little trip is just for Peach and me!"

"But - sir?" fluttered the White Linen Nurse. Her face was suddenly pinker than any rose that ever bloomed.

With an impulse absolutely novel to him the Senior Surgeon turned and swung his little daughter very gently to his shoulder.

"Your Aunt Agnes is coming to stay with *you* - in just about ten minutes!" he affirmed. "That's - what's going to happen to *you!* And maybe there'll be a pony - a white pony."

"But Peach is so - pleasant!" wailed the Little Crippled Girl. "Peach is so pleasant!" she began to scream and kick.

"So it seems!" growled the Senior Surgeon. "And she's - dying of it!"

Tearfully the Little Girl wriggled down to the ground, and hobbled around and thrust her finger-tip into the White Linen Nurse's blushiest cheek.

"I don't want - Peach - to - die," she admitted worriedly. "But I don't want anybody to take her away!"

"The pony is - very white," urged the Senior Surgeon with a diplomacy quite alien to him.

Abruptly the Little Girl turned and faced him. "What color is Aunt Agnes?" she asked vehemently.

"Aunt Agnes is - pretty white, too," attested the Senior Surgeon.

With the faintest possible tinge of superciliousness the Little Girl lifted her sharp chin a trifle higher.

"If it's just a perfectly plain white pony," she said, "I'd rather have Peach. But if it's a white pony with black blots on it, and if it can pull a little cart, and if I can whip it with a little switch, and if it will eat sugar-lumps out of my hand, - and if its name is - is - 'Beautiful Pretty-Thing' -"

"Its name has always been - 'Beautiful Pretty-Thing,' I'm quite sure!" insisted the Senior Surgeon. Inadvertently as he spoke he reached out and put a hand very lightly on the White Linen Nurse's shoulder.

Instantly into the Little Girl's suspicious face flushed a furiously uncontrollable flame of jealousy and resentment. Madly she turned upon her father.

"You're a liar!" she screamed. "There *is* no white pony! You're a robber! You're a - a - drunk! You shan't have my darling Peach!" And threw herself frenziedly into the White Linen Nurse's lap.

Impatiently the Senior Surgeon disentangled the little clinging arms, and raising the White Linen Nurse to her feet pushed her emphatically towards the hall.

"Go to my work-room," he said. "Quickly! I want to talk with you!"

A moment later he joined her there, and shut and locked the door behind him. The previous night's loss of sleep showed plainly in his face now, and the hospital strain of the day before, and of the day before that, and of the day before *that*.

Heavily, moodily, he crossed the room and threw himself down in his desk chair with the White Linen Nurse still standing before him as though she were nothing but a - white linen nurse. All the splendor was suddenly gone from him, all the radiance, all the exultant purpose.

"Well, Rae Malgregor," he grinned mirthlessly. "The little kid is right, though I certainly don't know where she got her information. I *am* a Liar. The pony's name is not yet 'Beautiful Pretty-Thing'! I *am* a - Drunk. I was drunk most of June! I *am* a Robber! I have taken you out of your youth - and the love-chances of your youth, - and shut you up here in this great, gloomy old house of mine - to be my slave - and my child's slave - and -"

"Pouf!" said the White Linen Nurse. "It would seem - silly - now, sir, - to marry a boy!"

"And I've been a beast to you!" persisted the Senior Surgeon. "From the very first day you belonged to me I've been a - beast to you, - venting brutally on your youth, on your sweetness, on your patience, - all the work, the worry, the wear and tear, the abnormal strain and stress of my disordered days - and years, - and I've let my little girl vent also on you all the pang and pain of *her* disordered days! And because in this great, gloomy, rackety house it seemed suddenly like a miracle from heaven to have service that was soft-footed, gentle-handed, pleasant-hearted, I've let you shoulder all the hideous drudgery, - the care, - one horrid homely task after another piling up-up-up - till you dropped in your tracks yesterday - still smiling!"

"But I got a good deal out of it, even so, sir!" protested the White Linen Nurse. "See, sir!" she smiled. "I've got real lines in my face - now - like other women! I'm not a doll any more! I'm not a -"

"Yes!" groaned the Senior Surgeon. "And I might just as kindly have carved those lines with my knife! But I was going to make it all up to you to-day!" he hurried. "I swear I was! Even in one short little week I could have done it! You wouldn't have known me! I was going to take you away, - just you and me! I would have been a Saint! I swear I would! I would have given you such a great, wonderful, child-hearted holiday - as you never dreamed of in all your unselfish life! A holiday all *you - you - you!* You could have - dug in the sand if you'd wanted to! Gad! I'd have dug in the sand - if you'd wanted me to! And now it's all gone from me, all the will, all the sheer positive self-assurance that I could have carried the thing through - absolutely selflessly. That little girl's sneering taunt? The ghost of her mother - in that taunt? God! When anybody knocks you just in your decency it doesn't harm you specially! But when they knock you in your Wanting-To-Be-Decent it - it undermines you somewhere. I don't know exactly how! I'm nothing but a man again - now, just a plain, every day, greedy, covetous, physical man - on the edge of a holiday, the first clean holiday in twenty years, - that he no longer dares to take!"

A little swayingly the White Linen Nurse shifted her standing weight from one foot to the other.

"I'm sorry, sir!" said the White Linen Nurse. "I'd like to have seen a roller-coaster, sir!"

Just for an instant a gleam of laughter went brightening across the Senior Surgeon's brooding face, and was gone again.

"Rae Malgregor, come here!" he ordered quite sharply.

Very softly, very glidingly, like the footfall of a person who has never known heels, the White Linen Nurse came forward swiftly and sliding in cautiously between the Senior Surgeon and his desk, stood there with her back braced against the desk, her fingers straying idly up and down the edges of the desk, staring up into his face all readiness, all attention, like a soldier waiting further orders.

So near was she that he could almost hear the velvet heart-throb of her, - the little fluttering swallow, - yet by some strange, persistent aloofness of her, some determinate virginity, not a fold of her gown, not an edge, not a thread, seemed to even so much as graze his knee, seemed to even so much as shadow his hand, - lest it short-circuit thereby the seething currents of their variant emotions.

With extraordinary intentness for a moment the Senior Surgeon sat staring into the girl's eyes, the blue, blue eyes too full of childish questioning yet to flinch with either consciousness or embarrassment.

"After all, Rae Malgregor," he smiled at last, faintly - "After all, Rae Malgregor, - Heaven knows when I shall ever get - another holiday!"

"Yes, sir?" said the White Linen Nurse.

With apparent irrelevance he reached for his ivory paper-cutter and began bending it dangerously between his adept fingers.

"How long have you been with me, Rae Malgregor?" he asked quite abruptly.

"Four months - actually with you, sir," said the White Linen Nurse.

"Do you happen to remember the exact phrasing of my - proposal of marriage to you?" he asked shrewdly.

"Oh, yes, sir!" said the White Linen Nurse. "You called it 'general heartwork for a family of two'!"

A little grimly before her steady gaze the Senior Surgeon's own eyes fell, and rallied again almost instantly with a gaze as even and direct as hers.

"Well," he smiled. "Through the whole four months I seem to have kept my part of the contract all right - and held you merely as a - drudge in my home. Have you then decided, once and for all time, - whether you are going to stay on with us - or whether you will 'give notice' as other drudges have done?"

With a little backward droop of one shoulder the White Linen Nurse began to finger nervously at the desk behind her, and turning half way round as though to estimate what damage she was doing, exposed thus merely the profile of her pink face, of her white throat, to the Senior Surgeon's questioning eyes.

"I shall never - give notice, sir!" fluttered the white throat.

"Are you perfectly sure?" insisted the Senior Surgeon.

The pink in the White Linen Nurse's profiled cheek deepened a little.

"Perfectly sure, sir!" attested the carmine lips.

Like the crack of a pistol the Senior Surgeon snapped the ivory paper cutter in two.

"All right then!" he said. "Rae Malgregor, look at me! Don't take your eyes from mine, I say! Rae Malgregor, if I should decide in my own mind, here and now, that it was best for you - as well as for me - that you should come away with me now - for this week, - not as my guest as I had planned, - but as my wife, - even if you were not quite ready for it in your heart, - even if you were not yet remotely ready for it, - would you come because I told you to come?"

Heavily under her white, white eyelids, heavily under her black, black lashes, the girl's eyes struggled up to meet his own.

"Yes, sir," whispered the White Linen Nurse.

Abruptly the Senior Surgeon pushed back his chair from the desk, and stood up. The important decision once made, no further finessing of words seemed either necessary or dignified to him.

"Go and pack your suit-case quickly then!" he ordered. "I want to get away from here within half an hour!"

But before the girl had half crossed the room he called to her suddenly, his whole bearing and manner miraculously changed, and his face in that moment as haggard as if a whole lifetime's struggle was packed into it.

"Rae Malgregor," he drawled mockingly. "This thing shall be - barter way through to the end, - with the credit always on your side of the account. In exchange for the gift - of yourself - your - wonderful self - and the trust that goes with it, I will give you, - God help me, - the ugliest thing in my life. And God knows I have broken faith with myself once or twice but - never have I broken my word to another! From now on, - in token of your trust in me, - for whatever the bitter gift is worth to you, - as long as you stay with me, - my Junes shall be yours - to do with - as you please!"

"What, sir?" gasped the White Linen Nurse. "*What*, sir?"

Softly, almost stealthily, she was half way back across the room to him, when she stopped suddenly and threw out her arms with a gesture of appeal and defiance.

"All the same, sir!" she cried passionately, "all the same, sir, - the place is too hard for the small pay I get! Oh, I will do what I promised!" she attested with increasing passion. "I will never leave you! And I will mother your little girl! And I will servant your big house! And I will go with you wherever you say! And I will be to you whatever you wish! And I will never flinch from any hardship you impose on me - nor whine over any pain, - on and on and on - all my days - all my years - till I drop in my tracks again and - die - as you say 'still smiling'! All the same!" she reiterated wildly, "the place is too hard! It always was too hard! It always will be too hard - for such small pay!"

"For such small pay?" gasped the Senior Surgeon.

Around his heart a horrid clammy chill began to settle. Sickeningly through his brain a dozen recent financial transactions began to rehearse themselves.

"You mean, Miss Malgregor," he said a bit brokenly. "You mean - that I - haven't been generous enough with you?"

"Yes, sir," faltered the White Linen Nurse.

All the storm and passion died suddenly from her, leaving her just a frightened girl again, flushing pink-white, pink-white, pink-white, before the Senior Surgeon's scathing stare. One step, two steps, three, she advanced towards him.

"Oh, I mean, sir," she whispered, "oh, I mean, sir, - that I'm just an ordinary, ignorant country girl and you - are further above me than the moon from the sea! I couldn't expect you to - love me, sir! I couldn't even dream of your loving me! *But I do think you might like me just a little bit with your heart!*"

"What?" flushed the Senior Surgeon. "*What?*"

Whacketty-bang against the window pane sounded the Little Crippled Girl's knuckled fists! Darkly against the window pane squashed the Little Crippled Girl's staring face.

"Father!" screamed the shrill voice. "Father! There's a white lady here with two black ladies washing the breakfast dishes! Is it Aunt Agnes?"

With a totally unexpected laugh, with a totally unexpected desire to laugh, the Senior Surgeon strode across the room and unlocked his door. Even then his lips against the White Linen Nurse's ear made just a whisper, not a kiss.

"God bless you! - *hurry!*" he said. "And let's get out of here before any telephone message catches me!"

Then almost calmly he walked out on the piazza, and greeted his sister-in-law.

"Hello, Agnes!" he said.

"Hello, yourself!" smiled his sister-in-law.

"How's everything?" he enquired politely.

"How's everything with you?" parried his sister-in-law.

Idly for a few moments the Senior Surgeon threw out stray crumbs of thought to feed the conversation, while smilingly all the while from her luxuriant East Indian chair his sister-in-law sat studying the general situation. The Senior Surgeon's sister-in-law was always studying something. Last year it was archaeology, - the year before, basketry, - this year it happened to be eugenics, or something funny like that, - next year again it might be book-binding.

"So you and your pink and white shepherdess are going off on a little trip together?" she queried banteringly. "The girl's a darling, Lendicott! I haven't had as much sport in a long time as I had that afternoon last June when I came in my best calling-clothes and - helped her paint the kitchen woodwork! And I had come prepared to be a bit nasty, Lendicott! In all honesty, Lendicott, I might just as well 'fess up that I had come prepared to be just a little bit nasty!"

"She seems to have a way," smiled the Senior Surgeon, "she seems to have a way of disarming people's unpleasant intentions."

A trifle quizzically for an instant the woman turned her face to the Senior Surgeon's. It was a worldly face, a cold-featured, absolutely worldly face, with a surprisingly humorous mouth that warmed her nature just about as cheer fully, and just about as effectually, as one open fireplace warms a whole house. Nevertheless one often achieved much comfort by keeping close to "Aunt Agnes's" humorous mouth, for Aunt Agnes knew a thing or two, - Aunt Agnes did, - and the things that she made a point of knowing were conscientiously amiable.

"Why, Lendicott Faber," she rallied him now. "Why, you're as nervous as a school-boy! Why, I believe - I believe that you're going courting!"

More opportunely than any man could have dared to hope, the White Linen Nurse appeared suddenly on the scene in her little blue serge wedding-suit with her traveling-case in her hand. With a gasp of relief the Senior Surgeon took her case and his own and went on down the path to his car and his chauffeur leaving the two women temporarily alone.

When he returned to the piazza the Woman-of-the-World and the Girl-not-at-all-of-the-World were bidding each other a really affectionate good-by, and the woman's face looked suddenly just a little bit old but the girl's cheeks were most inordinately blooming.

In unmistakable friendliness his sister-in-law extended her hand to him.

"Good-by, Lendicott, old man!" she said. "And good luck to you!" A little slyly out of her shrewd gray eyes, she glanced up sideways at him. "You've got the devil's own temper, Lendicott dear," she teased, "and two or three other vices probably, and if rumor speaks the truth you've run a-muck more than once in your life, - but there's one thing I will say for you, - though it prove you a dear Stupid: you never were over-quick to suspect that any woman could possibly be in love with you!"

"To what woman do you particularly refer?" mocked the Senior Surgeon impatiently.

Quite brazenly to her own heart which never yet apparently had stirred the laces that enshrined it, his sister-in-law pointed with persistent banter.

"Maybe I refer to - myself," she laughed, "and maybe to the

only - other lady present!"

"Oh!" gasped the White Linen Nurse.

"You do me much honor, Agnes," bowed the Senior Surgeon. Quite resolutely he held his gaze from following the White Linen Nurse's quickly averted face.

A little oddly for an instant the older woman's glance hung on his. "More honor perhaps than you think, Lendicott Faber!" she said, and kept right on smiling.

"Eh?" jerked the Senior Surgeon. Restively he turned to the White Linen Nurse.

Very flushingly on the steps the White Linen Nurse knelt arguing with the Little Crippled Girl.

"Your father and I are - going away," she pleaded. "Won't you - please - kiss us good-by?"

"I've only got one kiss," sulked the Little Crippled Girl.

"Give it to your - father!" pleaded the White Linen Nurse.

Amazingly all in a second the ugliness vanished from the little face. Dartlingly like a bird the Child swooped down and planted one large round kiss on the Senior Surgeon's astonished boot.

"Beautiful Father!" she cried, "I kiss your feet!"

Abruptly the Senior Surgeon plunged from the step and started down the walk. His cheek-bones were quite crimson.

Two or three rods behind him the White Linen Nurse followed falteringly. Once she stopped to pick up a tiny stick or a stone. And once she dallied to straighten out a snarled spray of red and brown woodbine.

Missing the sound or the shadow of her the Senior Surgeon turned suddenly to wait. So startled was she by his intentness, so flustered, so affrighted, that just for an instant the Senior Surgeon thought that she was going to wheel in her tracks and bolt madly back to the house. Then quite unexpectedly she gave an odd, muffled little cry, and ran swiftly to him like a child, and slipped her bare hand trustingly into his. And they went on together to the car.

With his foot already half lifted to the step the Senior Surgeon turned abruptly around and lifted his hat and stood staring back bareheaded for some unexplainable reason at the two silent figures on the piazza.

"Rae," he said perplexedly, "Rae, I don't seem to know just why - but somehow I'd like to have you kiss your hand to Aunt Agnes!"

Obediently the White Linen Nurse withdrew her fingers from his and wafted two kisses, one to "Aunt Agnes" and one to the Little Crippled Girl.

Then the White Linen Nurse and the Senior Surgeon climbed up into the tonneau of the car where they had never, never sat alone before, and the Senior Surgeon gave a curt order to his man and the big car started off again into - interminable spaces.

Mutely without a word, without a glance passing between them the Senior Surgeon held out his hand to her once more, as though the absence of her hand in his was suddenly a lonesomeness not to be endured again while life lasted.

Whizz - whizz - whizz - whirr - whirr - whirr the ribbony road began to roll up again on that hidden spool under the car.

When the chauffeur's mind seemed sufficiently absorbed in speed and sound the Senior Surgeon bent down a little mockingly and mumbled his lips inarticulately at the White

Linen Nurse.

"See!" he laughed. "I've got a text, too, to keep my courage up! Of course you look like an angel!" he teased closer and closer to her flaming face. "But all the time to myself - to reassure myself - I just keep saying - ' Bah! She 's nothing but a Woman - nothing but a Woman - nothing but a Woman'!"

Within the Senior Surgeon's warm, firm grasp the White Linen Nurse's calm hand quickened suddenly like a bud forced precipitously into full bloom.

"Oh, don't - talk, sir," she whispered. "Oh, don't talk, sir! Just - listen!"

"Listen? Listen to what?" laughed the Senior Surgeon.

From under the heavy lashes that shadowed the flaming cheeks the Soul of the Girl who was to be his peered up at the Soul of the Man who was to be hers, *- and saluted what she saw!*

"Oh, my heart, sir!" whispered the White Linen Nurse. "Oh, my heart! My heart! my *heart*!"

Choose from Thousands of 1stWorldLibrary Classics By

George Eliot
George Gissing
George MacDonald
George Meredith
George Orwell
George Sylvester Viereck
George Tucker
George W. Cable
George Wharton James
Gertrude Atherton
Gordon Casserly
Grace E. King
Grace Gallatin
Grace Greenwood
Grant Allen
Guillermo A. Sherwell
Gulielma Zollinger
Gustav Flaubert
H. A. Cody
H. B. Irving
H.C. Bailey
H. G. Wells
H. H. Munro
H. Irving Hancock
H. Rider Haggard
H. W. C. Davis
Haldeman Julius
Hall Caine
Hamilton Wright Mabie
Hans Christian Andersen
Harold Avery
Harold McGrath
Harriet Beecher Stowe
Harry Castlemon
Harry Coghill
Harry Houidini
Hayden Carruth
Helent Hunt Jackson
Helen Nicolay
Hendrik Conscience
Hendy David Thoreau
Henri Barbusse
Henrik Ibsen
Henry Adams
Henry Ford
Henry Frost
Henry James
Henry Jones Ford
Henry Seton Merriman
Henry W Longfellow
Herbert A. Giles
Herbert Carter
Herbert N. Casson
Herman Hesse
Hildegard G. Frey
Homer
Honore De Balzac
Horace B. Day
Horace Walpole
Horatio Alger Jr.
Howard Pyle
Howard R. Garis
Hugh Lofting
Hugh Walpole
Humphry Ward
Ian Maclaren
Inez Haynes Gillmore
Irving Bacheller
Isabel Hornibrook
Israel Abrahams
Ivan Turgenev
J.G.Austin
J. Henri Fabre
J. M. Barrie
J. Macdonald Oxley
J. S. Fletcher
J. S. Knowles
J. Storer Clouston
Jack London
Jacob Abbott
James Allen
James Andrews
James Baldwin
James Branch Cabell
James DeMille
James Joyce
James Lane Allen
James Lane Allen
James Oliver Curwood
James Oppenheim
James Otis
James R. Driscoll
Jane Austen
Jane L. Stewart
Janet Aldridge
Jens Peter Jacobsen
Jerome K. Jerome
John Burroughs
John Cournos
John F. Kennedy
John Gay
John Glasworthy
John Habberton
John Joy Bell
John Kendrick Bangs
John Milton
John Philip Sousa
Jonas Lauritz Idemil Lie
Jonathan Swift
Joseph A. Altsheler
Joseph Carey
Joseph Conrad
Joseph E. Badger Jr
Joseph Hergesheimer
Joseph Jacobs
Jules Vernes
Julian Hawthrone
Julie A Lippmann
Justin Huntly McCarthy
Kakuzo Okakura
Kenneth Grahame
Kenneth McGaffey
Kate Langley Bosher
Kate Langley Bosher
Katherine Cecil Thurston
Katherine Stokes
L. A. Abbot
L. T. Meade
L. Frank Baum
Latta Griswold
Laura Dent Crane
Laura Lee Hope
Laurence Housman
Lawrence Beasley
Leo Tolstoy
Leonid Andreyev
Lewis Carroll
Lewis Sperry Chafer
Lilian Bell
Lloyd Osbourne
Louis Hughes
Louis Tracy
Louisa May Alcott
Lucy Fitch Perkins
Lucy Maud Montgomery
Luther Benson
Lydia Miller Middleton
Lyndon Orr
M. Corvus
M. H. Adams
Margaret E. Sangster
Margret Howth
Margaret Vandercook

Margret Penrose
Maria Edgeworth
Maria Thompson Daviess
Mariano Azuela
Marion Polk Angellotti
Mark Overton
Mark Twain
Mary Austin
Mary Catherine Crowley
Mary Cole
Mary Hastings Bradley
Mary Roberts Rinehart
Mary Rowlandson
M. Wollstonecraft Shelley
Maud Lindsay
Max Beerbohm
Myra Kelly
Nathaniel Hawthrone
Nicolo Machiavelli
O. F. Walton
Oscar Wilde
Owen Johnson
P.G. Wodehouse
Paul and Mabel Thorne
Paul G. Tomlinson
Paul Severing
Percy Brebner
Peter B. Kyne
Plato
R. Derby Holmes
R. L. Stevenson
R. S. Ball
Rabindranath Tagore
Rahul Alvares
Ralph Bonehill
Ralph Henry Barbour
Ralph Victor
Ralph Waldo Emmerson
Rene Descartes
Rex Beach
Rex E. Beach
Richard Harding Davis
Richard Jefferies
Richard Le Gallienne
Robert Barr
Robert Frost
Robert Gordon Anderson
Robert L. Drake
Robert Lansing
Robert Lynd
Robert Michael Ballantyne
Robert W. Chambers
Rosa Nouchette Carey
Rudyard Kipling
Samuel B. Allison
Samuel Hopkins Adams
Sarah Bernhardt
Sarah C. Hallowell
Selma Lagerlof
Sherwood Anderson
Sigmund Freud
Standish O'Grady
Stanley Weyman
Stella Benson
Stella M. Francis
Stephen Crane
Stewart Edward White
Stijn Streuvels
Swami Abhedananda
Swami Parmananda
T. S. Ackland
T. S. Arthur
The Princess Der Ling
Thomas A. Janvier
Thomas A Kempis
Thomas Anderton
Thomas Bailey Aldrich
Thomas Bulfinch
Thomas De Quincey
Thomas Dixon
Thomas H. Huxley
Thomas Hardy
Thomas More
Thornton W. Burgess
U. S. Grant
Valentine Williams
Various Authors
Vaughan Kester
Victor Appleton
Victoria Cross
Virginia Woolf
Wadsworth Camp
Walter Camp
Walter Scott
Washington Irving
Wilbur Lawton
Wilkie Collins
Willa Cather
Willard F. Baker
William Dean Howells
William le Queux
W. Makepeace Thackeray
William W. Walter
William Shakespeare
Winston Churchill
Yei Theodora Ozaki
Yogi Ramacharaka
Young E. Allison
Zane Grey

www.ingramcontent.com/pod-product-compliance
Lightning Source LLC
LaVergne TN
LVHW090609110826
845146LV00001B/313

* 9 7 8 1 4 2 1 8 2 4 6 8 0 *